Oliver Pritchett was born in December 1939 and educated at Bryanston and Magdalen College, Oxford. He has been on the staff of the *Sunday Telegraph* since 1978 and, before that, worked for the *Observer*, the *Guardian* and the London *Evening Standard*. He was named General Feature Writer of the Year in the British Press Awards in 1981 and Commended in the Columnist of the Year category in 1992. His novel, *A Prize Paradise*, was published in 1979. He also broadcasts regularly on the BBC and has had a number of short stories published. He is married with two grown-up children, the cartoonist, Matt, and the comedy scriptwriter Georgia Pritchett. He lives in Kent.

The
Dogger Bank
Saga

Writings 1980–1995

by

OLIVER PRITCHETT

RICHARD COHEN BOOKS · London

British Library Cataloguing in Publication Data:
A catalogue record for this book
is available from the British Library

Copyright © 1995 *The Telegraph* plc

ISBN 1 86066 024 X

First published in Great Britain in 1995 by
Richard Cohen Books
7 Manchester Square
London W1M 5RE

Typeset in Linotron Imprint by
Rowland Phototypesetting Ltd,
Bury St Edmunds, Suffolk

Printed in Great Britain by
Clays Ltd, St Ives plc

Acknowledgements

The author would like to thank the *Daily Telegraph* and *Sunday Telegraph* in which all the pieces in this collection have previously appeared with the following exceptions: 'The Dogger Bank Saga' (formerly 'A General Synopsis'), 'There's Nowt So Queer as Folklore', 'Gardening Tips', 'Wash and Go' and 'The Magi Quiz' which are reprinted with kind permission of the BBC; and 'Bard of the Yard', courtesy of the *Evening Standard*.

Contents

JULY

AUGUST

SEPTEMBER

Introduction

SOME people want to make the break into serious journalism. They go to courses at the newer universities. They learn shorthand. They write up local soccer matches for free sheets, hoping that their style – a combination of Neville Cardus and Hugh McIlvanney ('like Cinderella, St Matthew's Juniors took an unconscionably long time getting to the ball') – will be noticed by a paper which is actually able to charge its readers. Their dream is that, one day, they will cover a train strike, or a Cabinet Minister's visit.

Oliver Pritchett has done the opposite. He has spent a career clawing his way out of serious journalism. His dream of a lifetime, which he finally realised only a few years ago, was that he would never again have to include a single fact in anything he wrote. His prose would become totally weightless, untethered by the surly bonds of earth, or indeed anything which might require checking.

It is a fine and noble aspiration. As I grow older I go to funerals and memorial services for former colleagues. At some point someone usually says: 'To dig out the facts, and to print them without comment or opinion, was all that he desired. He craved no title other than "reporter"; that was all the honour he wished to have.

Oliver has been the opposite. Years ago he realised that journalism filled with 'facts' was not only very misleading, offering a picture of the world quite unlike anything anyone recognised, but was also dreary and time-consuming. By ignoring facts altogether, he has been able, over the years, to furnish a more accurate picture of our national life than any number of news stories. Look back at the news pages of almost any paper of the 60's and 70's; you'll see lists of forgotten names, accounts of forgotten battles, acronyms of organisations which disappeared years ago. None of it means anything now. But read one of Oliver's pieces and the whole world returns to you, as powerful and pungent as the lost sights, smells and sounds of your childhood.

Oliver's struggle to free himself from facts began at the start of his career, working on the *Western Mail* in Cardiff. Here trainees were taught shorthand and newspaper law, both largely useless. If God had wanted us to learn either of these, He would not have invented tape recorders or lawyers. Oliver busied himself with misleading fashion tips, for example encouraging his readers to wear striped pyjama jackets as shirts.

Later he moved on to *Topic* magazine in London. This was owned for a time by a successful wide boy with political aspirations, who went on to become, under the name 'Michael Heseltine', Deputy Prime Minister and First Secretary of State.

Next he moved to the *Sunday Telegraph*, where he worked for the celebrated Kenneth Rose column. This still exists and is probably the least changed newspaper column in British history. If it were a folly in Stowe Landscape Gardens it would have a Grade I conservation order slapped on it. English Heritage would ban the changing of a single comma without their inspector's approval: 'Guests at the dedication of a new stained glass oriel window in the chapel of St. Strumpet's, Barchester, by Crown Prince Mikhail of Croatia this week may be interested to learn of an intriguing co-incidence. While a little girl, living at Strepps Castle, the Duchess of Monklands. . .'

This was followed by stints on the *Evening Standard* Londoner's Diary, and the Pendennis column of the *Observer*. After that Oliver moved to the *Guardian*, where, as he puts it, the Great Retreat from Reality got underway. He became – though there was no official title – the paper's roving trivia correspondent, covering marbles contests, snail races and competitions to discover Britain's Perfect Secretary. The *Guardian* was a very different paper in those days. Trivial subjects were treated with a certain ironic gravitas. Now serious topics are covered in Pass Notes, and the last vestiges of solemnity are reserved for reviews of rock CDs.

Then he went back to the *Standard*, and it was there that he began to write the sort of column collected in this book. (Even so, reality kept tugging him back, and the paper foolishly sent him off to cover by-elections and the like. On one occasion he was sent to interview Freddie Starr, the comedian who emphatically did *not* ever eat his girlfriend's hamster. Starr kept hitting him in what, at first, seemed a playful manner, but which was increasingly persistent and increasingly hard. Oliver suspects that this experience might have affected his brain.)

We had overlapped at the *Guardian*, though I was working in Northern Ireland, and it was on a brief visit to London that a friend showed me the *Evening Standard* column on policemen's poetry, which you will find in this collection. The clipping was beginning to fall to pieces, since she had kept it in her address book, neatly folded, much read and well thumbed. I thought it was perfect, and still do. I was also deeply envious. Any fool can write amusingly about MPs, since your subjects do most of the work for you, but to create your own topic and be hilarious about that is a talent given to very few.

He returned to the *Sunday Telegraph*, where various executives with poor judgement would send him off to write about strikes and other ephemera. We both covered Margaret Thatcher's first victorious election campaign. Few who were there will forget that magical moment somewhere in the Midlands when she picked up a new-born calf and brandished it at the camera. Denis Thatcher uttered the quintessential Denis Thatcher line: 'if we're not careful, we're going to have a dead calf on our hands.'

But after a while they gave him half of the humour slot on the editorial pages, alternating fortnightly with the late Arthur Marshall. The column was so funny and so popular that it soon went weekly, and in 1986 a second began in the *Daily Telegraph*, on Tuesdays.

In the early 90's I began to work on a Radio 4 programme called Fourth Column. This was meant to be a radio version of *Punch*, which was then in what proved to be terminal decline, having been taken over by unimaginably stupid marketing persons and 'yoof'. I asked Oliver if he had any ideas, and the first he came up with was the Shipping Forecast piece, which appears in print here for the first time and gives the book its title.

This particular column, which was broadcast for the first time in 1991, may be the most repeated single item on BBC Radio of the past ten years. It has been on Fourth Column, Pick of the Week (and its repeat), the Best of Fourth Column, Fourth Column Classics, Pick of the Year (and repeat); in short, there was a period when it was hard to switch on your radio and not hear the Shipping Forecast being read in Oliver's distinctive voice, which combines hesitancy with a certain lugubrious charm. Many of Fourth's Column's finest moments were provided by Oliver, such as the wonderful Three Wise Men's Christmas Quiz, which is also in this book.

Personal details now: Oliver is the son of Sir Victor Pritchett and he is the father of Matt, the *Telegraph*'s superlative pocket cartoonist. His daughter Georgia used to be our nanny when we lived in America, but now is one of the most successful young comedy script writers. The family is sodden with talent. It's as if they won the jackpot in the National Lottery for Comic Skills.

Oliver and his wife live in a village in Kent in a house so small that in a hundred years there will be no room for the plaque on the wall. However, it has one of the best pubs I know. Once we visited the Pritchetts for Sunday lunch, and the innkeeper served us a vast dish of roast potatoes with Cumberland sausage. I had assumed this was lunch, but it was merely a snack - what passes for an *amuse-gueule* in those parts.

In the days of the old Fleet Street a Pritchett column might be born in the back room of the new El Vino's, by Blackfriars Bridge, with the whole school tossing ideas in the pot. Since the British press has been dispersed/this is no longer possible, and Oliver generally starts a new piece by walking round the village. One complete circuit per paragraph; the whole thing is mentally written in about three miles. The other villagers are used to him, and leave him alone with his thoughts; he's particularly grateful that they will stop their dogs barking at him. The dogs are inclined to bark because Oliver is not the world's neatest dresser. He favours woolly, cordy, tweedy clothes, and looks like an American academic fallen on hard times.

And the question he's always asked: where do the ideas come from? Recycled anxiety, he says, taking the worry and working on it. Here then are a collection of the funniest fears in British journalism.

January

1

The Dogger Bank Saga

People often ask me how I get my ideas for the hugely success-ful TV drama series I write. As it happens I do know exactly where and when it was that I got the inspiration for my latest blockbuster.

It is one of those sagas about two great dynasties in Texas and the whole thing came to me at ten-to-six last Thursday evening. I know the precise time because I was listening to Radio Four. By the time the weather forecast came on at five-to-six I had the whole thing mapped out.

I'll give you a general synopsis. It is about these two adjoin-ing cattle ranches – North Utsire and South Utsire. North Utsire is the home of the Tyne family and they have a herd of pedigree Sumburgh cattle. The patriarch of the family, living in a tastelessly furnished mansion, is old Dogger Tyne. He is rough and tough, has white hair and also blue eyes which he crinkles up meaningfully. He is widowed and has two daughters. The youngest is Lundy who is pert and tom-boyish. The other daughter, Valentia, is quite different. She wears a lot of lip gloss and her lustrous head of hair is so heavily lacquered that it hardly moves when she goes out in a high wind – even Gale 8 at times.

Old Dogger Tyne loathes the Fisher family at South Utsire. The head of this family is Cromarty Fisher. He is fair, moder-ate and good. He has a senior ranch hand called Lewis whom he treats like a brother. Sometimes, however, he asserts his authority and kicks the butt of Lewis.

Cromarty Fisher has a handsome son named Rockall who has a hyperactive Adam's Apple, denoting sensitivity. Of course, Rockall Fisher is in love with Lundy Tyne.

Why, you ask, do the Tynes hate the Fishers? It goes back

to an earlier generation when Viking Tyne was courting the wistful, romantic Faeroes Fisher, but the families would not let them marry. Poor Faeroes went mad and threw herself off a cliff. The wind was Storm force 10 at the time. Viking died of grief. (All this can be seen in flashback.) Some folks say Faeroes secretly gave birth to a daughter called Hebrides. (She will turn up as a successful lawyer in Episode Fourteen.)

Other characters include Dogger Tyne's sidekick, a sinister figure called Malin. He owns a fierce dog – a German Bight. He seldom speaks, just gives the odd, intermittent light scowl.

Then there is the femme fatale, Shannon Fastnet, who is in love with Rockall Fisher but knows it is hopeless. She drives her scarlet Portland convertible too fast and she goes to the bars in the nearby town of Biscay where she drinks too many potent Bell Rock cocktails.

You will soon be seeing the whole drama on your TV screens and I don't want to spoil the plot for you. I will just mention one marvellously dramatic moment. Young Lundy Tyne is being blackmailed by the evil Malin and finally she can take no more. She pulls out a Smiths Knoll Automatic and shoots at him. Malin just laughs in his sinister way. 'Missed,' he sneers. 'Three miles.'

2

The rain it raineth every day – official

Tomorrow is Twelfth Night. Hooray. It is a marvellous occasion, when we find our sitting-rooms festooned with charming little pieces of sticky tape, which were used to hold up the decorations.

It is a time when we can finally put away those Christmas cards which have been falling off the mantelpiece for the past three weeks. The withered and wrinkled balloons can now be put out of their misery.

I have never really felt that Shakespeare did justice to the special qualities of this time, in his play *Twelfth Night*. There is no mention in the text, for example, of throwing away the last four gallons of turkey broth. No reference to how long the shops in Illyria remained closed during the holiday period, no scene in which a leading character transfers old telephone numbers to his new diary. I have adapted the play to incorporate the true flavour of *Twelfth Night* . . .

In the first scene, we see Duke Orsino's Palace. The message 'Merry Christmas' sprayed on to an upper window can be read from the outside. The final letter 's' has been carelessly reversed. This is because Orsino is distracted as he is hopelessly in love with the haughty Olivia, who refused to come to his New Year's Eve mulled wine party.

The play opens with Orsino's memorable line: 'If music be the food of love, play that cassette of Bing Crosby's *Greatest Yuletide Hits* once more before we put it away for another year.'

Orsino's household is joined by Viola, who has been stranded in Illyria, because of the disruption to British Rail timetables. As her office is closed anyway until the middle of January, she decides to disguise herself as a youth called

Cesario, and do odd jobs for the Duke, who sends her as a kissogram to Olivia.

At Olivia's house we find Sir Toby Belch and Sir Andrew Aguecheek who went to an office party on December 9, and have been in no fit state ever since. They have not quite finished their bottle of ghastly creamy liqueur, and they still have a few Panatellas left from a gift pack of 100.

Olivia is scraping the little triangles of artificial snow from the bottom corners of her window panes, when Cesario (alias Viola) arrives. She is immediately smitten by love.

Meanwhile Malvolio is still puzzling over a Christmas card he received showing an attractive coaching scene. The message inside is warm and tender, but he cannot decipher the signature. 'I wonder if I sent her one,' he ponders.

Belch and Aguecheek persuade him that it is from Olivia, and also deceive him into thinking she has invited him to a fancy dress party. When he shows up cross-gartered, she is extremely cross because it is supposed to be a working breakfast to review plans for the coming year.

Malvolio appears to go mad, writhing about and moaning. It turns out that he simply has several pine needles from the Christmas tree stuck inside his shirt.

Fortunately Viola's brother, Sebastian, arrives on the scene, and a potentially explosive love-tangle situation is averted.

Everyone rejoices that the Christmas season is over, and that television programmes are back to normal again. They switch on the set for the weather forecast, and Michael Fish (a clown) sings: 'With a hey, ho, the wind and the rain . . . for the rain it raineth every day'.

3

When help is close at hand

Who, in 1991, said this? 'All right, I don't know the answer, but it is a pretty stupid question anyway.' Actually, I did. I said it while I was still fretting away at a 1990 Christmas quiz. It was shortly afterwards that I decided to set up my counselling service for the victims of Christmas quizzes.

This season has turned into an annual festival of general knowledge. It has become an excuse for the abstruse. There are quizzes everywhere, in every newspaper and magazine to fill space and time between now and the New Year. This can be a period of agony for those unfortunate people who don't know the name of the longest river in Paraguay and have forgotten who won the bronze medal for the long jump in the Seoul Olympics. The collective noun for okapi is, alas, still stuck on the tip of their tongues.

These people face embarrassment and humiliation. The first important thing we must do is change public attitudes. A person who does not know, for example, the precise height of Mont Blanc should not be called ignorant; he is just 'factually challenged'.

I once knew a perfectly respectable quantity surveyor whose career was ruined after he was arrested while breaking into a public library on Boxing Day.

He wanted to look up Goethe's middle name and was caught by an off-duty policeman who had gone there to try and find out the capital of Chad. (The tragic irony is that the policeman knew Goethe's middle name and my friend knew the capital of Chad. But this did not emerge until after the trial.)

As part of my counselling duties, I go to visit a poor fellow who is still suffering the after-effects of the *Spectator* Christmas Quiz of 1988. He has recurring nightmares that he is

7

appearing on *Mastermind* and discovers he is stark naked and has chosen the History of the Universe as his specialist subject.

There are others who suffer from long-term self-disgust because they looked up the quiz answers. You often see them reading their newspaper or magazine upside down as a sort of public display of their shame.

With these quiz victims we tried to help them win back their self-respect and to convince them that just because they do not know the name of the Belgian minister of education they are not entirely worthless. We teach them to say: 'I'm afraid I do not know that but, if you like, I can stand on one leg with a packet of frozen peas balanced on my head and whistle selections from the Mikado at the same time.'

For this counselling work, we have taken over a house in Herne Bay which was, in the old days, a convalescent home for people recovering from painful family games of Monopoly. We teach them how to take evasive action when faced with a quiz. There is also a 24-hour Helpline with thirty volunteers armed with reference books ready to help you bluff your way through any quiz. Unfortunately, I have forgotten the telephone number for the moment, but know there is a 4 in it. And a 0 and perhaps a 3.

We also have a Jumbo Crossword Support Group (with anagram aversion therapy) and we offer shelter to anyone on the run from Trivial Pursuit. In fact, this Christmas we are hoping to provide comfort not only for quiz victims, but also for people who can't begin to understand the rules of the new board game they have been given, who can't get beyond the title page of their computer user's handbook and who are baffled when the assembly instructions for the build-your-own nuclear power station kit say 'slide stud of flange Q into slotted template R'. They will all be welcome in our retreat and reassured by our motto – No Questions Asked.

4

1788 and all that

Today is Australia Day. However cool the Australians themselves may appear to be about us and about their bicentenary, we back here are passionate antipodophiles.

The history of Australia is straightforward. Basically what happened is that Britain sent out a lot of convicts 200 years ago and, as soon as they had begun to settle down, we sent out a cricket team to bowl very fast at their heads. The Australians wore a protective armour of corks dangling from the brims of their hats and were relatively unscathed. Ned Kelly kept scoring centuries against England and Sir Donald Bradman was made Prime Minister.

Before the first settlers arrived in Australia there were Aborigines. They were persecuted for going walkabout looking for their boomerangs and singing songlines. Now they live in dreadful conditions – reduced to being the subject matter of gloomy television documentaries by John Pilger.

The geography of the place is quite simple, too. The country consists of a large stretch of beach where suntanned surfers wrestle with crocodiles and barbecue sharks; then there is an opera house which looks as if it is going to topple over at any moment and a large area of suburbs that has been built so that expatriate Australians can make a living in London by mocking them.

There is also something called the Outback, which is arid. It contains a big dingo-infested rock to which people like to go to watch the sun rise.

All place names in Australia end in 'agga' or 'oo' or 'ong' except the capital city which is called A Town Like Alice.

A long, absolutely straight railway line goes right through the centre of Australia, stopping at sheep stations to unload cans of beer. As for the climate, the only essential fact to remember is that it is always sweltering hot on Christmas Day.

Social conditions in Australia are excellent. They do not have problems like ours with the National Health Service. Indeed, all Australian doctors have a private aeroplane. Most of the rest of the population are newspaper proprietors, although there are also a few people in the country who make a good living by writing memoirs of their life with MI5.

Crime in Australia is virtually unknown, apart from the slight risk of being mugged if you are unwise enough to camp by a billabong. (A billabong is a sort of dance hall specialising in the waltz.)

It sounds a wonderful country. And you can tell how hooked we are on it by the fact that around about 14 million people here now watch the second-rate Australian television soap opera, *Neighbours*.

Personally, I would certainly emigrate there if it were not for the fact that I would miss certain essential ingredients of British culture, such as Dame Edna Everage, Clive James, Germaine Greer and even Rolf Harris.

5

Yes, but how does the poor old bargain feel about being hunted?

The bargain hunting season is now in full swing, with not just the January sales but also the supermarkets' price war, the travel industry's special offers and, of course, the trips across the Channel for cheap alcohol and tobacco. Bargain hunting is one of this country's colourful traditions. It is a marvellous sight, on a wintry morning, to see a 'meet' in the car park of some store. There they are, with their garish plastic carrier bags or their shopping trolleys in the tartans of the famous consumer clans, such as 'the haggling Robinsons' or the 'bulk-buying Bennetts'.

They are snorting and champing at the bit, waiting to be let into the store; steam rises from them in the frosty air. They fortify themselves with plastic cups of milky coffee from vacuum flasks; you can hear the jingle of their purses and see the pale sun glinting on their shiny credit cards.

Then at last the MBH (Master of the Bargain Hunt) gives the signal to move on. He shouts 'Twenty-two per cent off!' and they all gallop into the store. The MBH is also accompanied by the 'nippers-in' – these are the lithe and nimble people who can squirm to the front of a crowd at the counter, nip in and snatch a bargain from under somebody else's nose.

After them come the followers on foot, usually known as Kylie or Jason, whose unmistakable howls and wails can be heard from soft furnishings to electrical appliances.

There is nothing to beat the thrill of the sight of a pack of bargain hunters thundering down one of the beautifully laid-out aisles of Sainsbury's in full cry and in pursuit of rump steak which has been reduced to £2.58 per lb.

When I see a bargain hunt move off I am often reminded

of John Beale, perhaps the greatest bargain hunter of all. His many brilliant feats in running special offers to earth are still recounted. It is said that he waited outside Selfridges, in Oxford Street, for three days and nights in order to buy a tumble drier for £39.99. You probably recall the words of the old song: 'D'ye ken John Beale when he's far far away at the front of the queue in the morning?'

Of course, bargain hunting does have its opponents. The people who go across to Calais to buy several cases of cheap insipid Continental beer may rightly be described by admirers of Oscar Wilde as 'the unspeakable in full pursuit of the undrinkable'. Actually, it takes a good deal of courage to go hunting for bargains. Many people have come a nasty cropper through a failure of negotiation in a clearance sale, or have come down to earth with a nasty bump after a hard day's shopping.

Some people object to bargain hunting for reasons of class. They think it is an occupation solely for loud-mouthed red-faced toffs. It is true that some rather tiresome upper crust folk tend to boast that they 'hunt with the Harrods', but there are plenty of famous hunts that could hardly be called snobbish – like the Tesco or the MFI. There is nothing to beat that feeling, when you come home at the end of the day, weary and battered, but with a sense of achievement with your 'bargain pack'.

Some people say bargain hunting is cruel and argue that it

should be banned altogether. I think this would be a regrettable move. Although I certainly do not go as far as those people who claim that the bargain actually *enjoys* being hunted, I believe abolition would spoil the pleasure of a lot of people. It would not just affect those who like to have a day out with the Harrods or the Fenwicks or the Harvey Nichols, but it would also spoil the pleasure of the ordinary man or woman who goes out in the hope of picking up a cauliflower or a shoulder of lamb on special offer, or two pence off a packet of tea.

And, of course, I have absolutely no time for the extremists of the so-called 'bargain hunt saboteurs', who jam the wheels of supermarket trolleys in a way that can be dangerous, or go into the shops and switch all the price labels in an attempt to put the hunters off the scent of a bargain.

These saboteurs have no understanding of the way of life in the big chain stores. They are all hypocrites; they say bargain hunting is barbaric, but they see nothing wrong in rummaging around in jumble sales.

6

The screen is our oyster

A surge in holiday bookings for Corsica is predicted, simply because Chief Inspector Wexford was seen there in a *Ruth Rendell Murder Mystery* on ITV over Christmas. Florida hoteliers are breathing sighs of relief because the Trotter family went there in an episode of *Only Fools and Horses*. This is how tourism works, according to the travel agents. If we are not in Herriot country, you will find us in Jersey looking for Bergerac, or we may follow Shirley Valentine to Mykonos.

Not long ago, I was at the Parthenon, in Athens, which, as you know, was 'put on the map' by the television series *Above the Line*, about a glamorous international syndicate of troubleshooting chartered accountants.

'It is amazing to think,' I said at the time, 'that I am standing on the very spot where Irene turned down a marriage proposal from Rex because she wanted to pursue her career as an acupuncturist, little knowing that Rex would soon be in a coma after being hit by a thick ledger, hurled by the insanely jealous Samantha. If only these old stones could speak, what tales they would tell about the filming of that episode!'

If the television companies are so good at promoting package tours, perhaps they should go into the tourist business more wholeheartedly. Not just adventure hols with Kate Adie, but wildlife safaris with David Attenborough and perhaps also an *Antiques Roadshow Mystery Tour*, during which your personable and well-informed courier says: 'Would it surprise you to hear that this holiday is going to cost you in the region of £5,000?'

The most exciting prospect would be if the Association of British Travel Agents took it a step further and went into the business of making television programmes. I have jotted down a few ideas. We could have a drama series called *Ten Days in Torremolinos*, a title that suggests both glamour and menace. Then, perhaps, *No Surcharges*. This is a tough thriller, featuring Tim 'Golden' Sands, the fair-haired secret agent with eyes the colour of the water in the kidney-shaped swimming pool at the Hotel Paradise in Barbados. There could also be a sit-com about a Nottingham family and their hilarious exploits in Brittany. This would be called *Pardon My Gîte*.

You can recognise the beauty of the idea of ABTA television programmes if you just consider the photographs in the brochures. You always want to know what happens next. There is this couple sitting rather woodenly in semi darkness on stools at a rickety bar, and you cannot help feeling that an extraordinary drama must have unfolded five seconds after that photograph was taken. The caption simply says 'Sophisticated Nightlife'.

Let us take a closer look at those brochures. We see a couple seated at a table under a thatched sunshade on the beach. Something is up. You can tell that by their fixed smiles and the way they are not actually looking at each other. This is how I see the plot: the bright red cocktail in the woman's glass with all the fruit and the paper umbrella and the straw is, in fact, a poison prepared by the man in the picture who may be her husband. He has noticed that just behind her left shoulder the picturesque native fishermen in loincloths are hauling in their nets which, they are about to discover, contain the body of the man's first wife whom he stabbed with a kebab skewer, taken from the hotel's restaurant, which is noted for its international cuisine.

Now for the twist in the plot. We thought the woman was poisoned, but here she is, a few pages further on in the brochure, wearing the same yellow bikini, but now lounging by a swimming pool in Torquay. She has acquired two teenage children. Great heavens! Here is the husband looking round Rheims cathedral with an entirely different partner. What is going on? Has the woman in the yellow bikini got a twin sister? Is it time for Chief Inspector Wexford to arrive for an off-season break? I'll have to get away somewhere to find the inspiration to finish this script. Maybe to Tuscany. John Mortimer country, you know.

7

This is a library fine romance

Historical romances, it was reported last week, are the most popular books in public libraries. Authors of these works are the highest earners under the Public Lending Right, based on the number of borrowings. The answer is to write a historical romance set in a public library. I have now done so. The book is called *The Overdue Heart*.

Shortly after breakfast Belinda Temple-Meads put on her bonnet and her driving cloak and left Nuneaton Manor in a barouche to travel to the public library. As the horses clattered into the cobblestoned courtyard of the library she remembered the injunction of her dear papa – 'A maximum of six books may be borrowed at any time.'

Although she was only seventeen, Belinda had a wise head on her shoulders and honey-coloured ringlets tumbling down her neck. She felt a tremor of anticipation as she approached the fiction shelves.

She knew what she sought: the S section and the volumes by Hortense Sweetbriar. She would borrow *Proud Enchantress*, but she would also take out *Mistress of Eastling Hall* for her new, dear, sweet-natured companion Thérèse, who was too unwell to accompany her to the library.

When she reached the shelf she was dumbfounded to discover that all the books by Hortense Sweetbriar were missing. There was not even a copy of *Proclaim it at Midnight*.

Belinda ran blindly across the room to the desk of the chief librarian, the Comtesse de Microfiche, who had recently made a daring escape from the revolutionary mobs in Paris. 'My child, why are your eyes stinging with angry tears?' the Comtesse inquired kindly. Belinda blurted out her dismay at the missing books.

'The answer to the mystery lies over there,' said the Comtesse pointing in the direction of the non-fiction section. A tall gentleman with an aloof manner was standing studying a volume intently.

'His name is Darlington Stockton, and he has not long ago returned from the colonies, where he is reputed to have accumulated a huge fortune. He has borrowed all the Hortense Sweetbriar books and refuses to return them. He has now accumulated a huge sum in fines. I believe he is incapable of loving.'

At that moment the man walked purposefully to the desk, taking long strides and borrowing a copy of *Practical Caravan Maintenance* by T. G. Whitaker. As he was waiting for the book to be date-stamped he turned to Belinda and said, 'That is a very becoming gown.' There was amusement in his eyes, which were an unusual shade of green. Belinda nodded coolly with chilly reserve.

After Mr Stockton had left, the Comtesse said: 'He comes here every day. He borrows *Practical Caravan Maintenance*, then returns it, then borrows it again immediately.'

The next day Belinda arrived at the library again. 'I can see that you are tilting your chin defiantly and that you intend to challenge Mr Stockton about the missing books,' the Comtesse said. Belinda flushed.

A few moments later she found herself accosting Mr Stockton. 'I must request you, sir, to return *Proud Enchantress* at your earliest convenience,' she exclaimed.

'Those books are nothing but sentimental rubbish,' Mr Stockton retorted brusquely. At this moment Miss Shelf, the severe assistant librarian and former governess to a titled family, arrived at his side. 'I must ask you not to retort brusquely or laugh sardonically,' she said, 'as this disturbs other library users.' Mr Stockton frowned and Belinda could not meet his eyes.

She turned to Miss Shelf. 'This gentleman is attempting to pervert the Public Lending Right system,' she accused. 'He is borrowing *Practical Caravan Maintenance* over and over again in order to enrich its author, T. G. Whitaker, while he is keeping the works of Hortense Sweetbriar out of circulation, thus depriving her of income that is rightfully hers.'

17

Mr Stockton turned to Belinda with a grave look. 'You must think me very heartless,' he said. 'But please hear me out. When I was very young, my mother died. My poor sister Thérèse was sent to an orphanage while I was fostered by a wealthy family in Northamptonshire. Recently I learned that she was the T. G. Whitaker who wrote *Practical Caravan Maintenance*, so I decided to support her discreetly by borrowing the book many times. It meant depriving Hortense Sweetbriar, but I could afford that.'

'So my dear, sweet friend Thérèse is your sister and *you* are Hortense Sweetbriar!' exclaimed Belinda falling headlong in love.

'Please do not throw yourselves into each other's arms, half-laughing and half-crying,' said Miss Shelf, 'as this disturbs other library users.'

February

8

Cochonette chérie, let's form a joint social partnership

It is strange to think that this is the last traditional Valentine's Day before the new European Union regulations come into force in 1996. Obviously, February 14 will still be important, but in a different form.

The British greeting card industry is gearing itself up for the changes, which may, in fact, turn out to be a blessing in disguise, according to government sources. The main difference is that it will no longer be permitted to put a heart symbol on cards. This is a result of a directive from the EU Agriculture Commission, implementing a clause in the treaty concerning the depiction of offal.

When Britain signed up to this treaty in 1989 it was thought that it just covered advertisements for tripe, liver and sweetbreads, and so on, but it recently emerged that the rule included hearts on Valentine cards. The new EU directive states that any pictorial representation of offal – such as hearts, livers, kidneys etc – must include printed information on what beast it comes from, when the beast was slaughtered and the code number of the veterinary authority which inspected the carcass. The depiction must also be 'true to life' – so that also rules out the traditional heart symbol.

Mr Herbert Pash, the junior Home Office minister with special responsibility for meaningful relationships, is said to have fought Britain's corner valiantly over this issue at the negotiations in Lisbon last September, and he won important concessions.

He came back with an acceptable deal on the question of trees on which lovers' hearts and arrows have been carved. Under a special opt-out, we shall not have to complete the programme of felling these trees until 1998, though such

21

symbols will still have to be removed from the walls of school buildings before the beginning of the next academic year.

In return for these concessions, any Spanish male under the age of eighty-five is allowed to come to Britain and have unlimited access to declare his love to any resident British female.

The expression 'roses are red, violets are blue' is to be phased out by January 9 next year. This is to bring Britain into line with the thinking in other European countries on the question of floral pigmentation. It has been forcefully pointed out to Douglas Hurd on many occasions that calling violets blue is misleading; violets are, in fact, violet – and sometimes white. It was widely felt among our EU partners that the Foreign Office was dragging its feet by insisting on the blueness of violets.

A powerful lobby of Belgian growers of yellow roses brought its influence to bear on the negotiations, and then the influential Committee for Colour Blind Affairs in the European Parliament also made representations.

So, the final, approved version of the poetic lines now reads: 'Roses come in a wide variety of colours, including many attractive shades of yellow; violets are violet or white, but not necessarily.' I understand that representatives of the British greeting card industry are appealing to the Government for a £30 million grant for research into words that rhyme with 'not necessarily'.

All pet names used in Valentine's messages must be registered on a computer in Dusseldorf at least three months before next February 14. This is to avoid misunderstandings and embarrassments resulting from any duplication.

Last night Mr Pash issued a statement saying: 'Britain has taken a leading role in the EU development of expressions of amorous sentiment. We can be proud of our record.'

Now the Foreign Office is preparing for the Inter-Governmental Conference on Kissing which takes place in Athens next year. The conference arises from the need to harmonise social kissing and to settle, once and for all, whether a social kiss should consist of one, two, or even three pecks on the cheek. Confusion in the past has led to unintentional head-butting at EU summits.

The French and the Germans are keen for the scope of the conference to be widened and to include 'all aspects of osculatory activity'. Mr Hurd has let it be known that he expects Britain to pucker her weight on this one.

Euro-sceptics are warning that, if we concede one more peck, Britain will never be able to extricate herself from the EU embrace.

9

Cupid speaks frankly for the first time

Cupid received me in his spacious but unpretentious ninth-floor office. He hardly ever gives interviews, but he made an exception on this occasion for Valentine's Day. There were, of course, some ground rules; his own love-life was strictly a no-go area. Apart from that, I found him remarkably relaxed and open.

'Oh, yes, I work out a bit,' Cupid said. 'Well, you have to in this job. It takes a lot out of you, hovering four feet above the ground, fluttering your wings, pulling on a bow, aiming and trying to keep your little bit of loincloth on, all at the same time. And it takes co-ordination.'

'There have been suggestions that your arrows some-times hit the wrong person,' I said. Cupid ruffled his wing feathers in a gesture of impatience. 'There is no point in dwelling on past mistakes. The important thing is to move forward. As far as the bow and arrows are concerned, I believe great strides have been made in targeting the individual correctly.'

Following complaints that Cupid has been exercising arbitrary powers, shooting arrows almost at random and making people fall in love without even allowing them any right of appeal, there are now thought to be moves to make him more answerable. Some people have said that he is too remote from the lives of ordinary people. This is probably why he agreed to grant me an interview.

I asked him about his mother, Venus. 'I'll admit it was a bit of a problem for me, having this world-famous sex goddess for a mum,' he said. 'All those stories about her and her heart-shaped swimming-pool, all the parties, and so on. Yes, it did freak me sometimes. That could be why I started eating too much, not watching my weight and putting the arrows about in a careless manner.'

Cupid told me he was considering making some changes in his methods. 'Up to now there has been a problem with the absence of back-up,' he said. 'I'd like to see a system where I shoot my arrows, then the people who are smitten are visited by counsellors and helped to cope with their new situation as lovers. The aftercare side has been sadly neglected.'

Valentine's Day for Cupid will be 'just a normal working day'. He will be out with his bow and arrows and shooting at the people who are on a list that has been drawn up by his research unit. 'There is still the random element, of course,' he said. 'Otherwise it would be no fun. We just like to avoid the obvious mistakes, such as making a non-smoker fall in love with a smoker.'

As our interview came to an end Cupid opened a bottle of dry white wine and relaxed, lounging elegantly on the ceiling. 'You know, in this job, one gets a lot of criticism when a relationship goes wrong,' he said. 'It's just something you have to learn to live with. At the end of the day, all I can say is: 'I aim to please.'

10

Out of the frying pan

Pancake Day is particularly exciting this year because this is the first time it has been fully integrated into the EC Calendar of Traditional and Folkloric Occasions for Merrymaking, known as CATFOM, or, if you are in France COMFAT.

As our pancakes are now, as they say, well and truly 'in Europe', certain adjustments have been made to the celebration of Pancake Day. Of course, as you will know from the leaflet delivered to every household in the country, the making of pancakes now comes under the Crêpes Suzette safety regulations directive of 1989. Statistics compiled by the committee headed by Dr Otto Feuereimer, a senior EC Hazards Officer, indicated that in the last decade several people (thought to be as many as nine) had suffered minor singes from flaming Crêpes Suzette and as many again had burned their tongues on the hot sauce.

After the report of the committee, Crêpes Suzette were categorised, along with rhubarb crumble and custard, as 'puddings involving unacceptable risk'. The regulations were phased in and were fully implemented last year making it an offence for anyone to cook Crêpes Suzette in their own home.

They can, of course, still be prepared in restaurants where they come under the terms of the Combustible Comestibles Accord of 1986, which was ratified at the 1987 Treaty of Padua. This governs the preparation of all dishes which waiters feel it necessary to *flambé* rather flamboyantly at the table.

Some *Daily Telegraph* readers may be a bit rusty on the subject of the 1987 Treaty of Padua and the Combustible Comestibles Accord, but I would warmly recommend them to re-read the leaflet on the subject that was delivered to all households in October 1988. Otherwise they might find themselves in the position of the Solihull woman who was fined £30,000 for setting fire to a Christmas pudding last year and whose appeal is still being considered by the European Court of Justice and could take another seventeen years.

Incidentally, although Britain was a reluctant signatory of the Combustible Comestibles Accord we did some hard bargaining and won a major concession: the clause requiring a fire brigade appliance to be present at all barbecues attended by more than five people does not come into effect in this country until June 1993.

Now, back to Pancake Day. Although the traditional British pancake is not usually set alight, it is, for the purpose of the drafting of the regulations, identical to the Crêpes Suzette. The two have been, as it were, lumped together. Therefore, today, these rules apply: pancakes may be prepared only in a public place specifically licensed for the purpose and written permission must be obtained, at least three weeks in advance, from the Crêpes Suzette Licensing Authority – the CSLA, or, in France, the ALCS.

Of course, there is no need for me to tell anyone who is the slightest bit *au fait* with the Calendar of Traditional and Folkloric Occasions for Merrymaking that actually tossing the pancake is quite out of the question. Apart from the obvious hazards involved, there is also (because of the egg content of the batter) the risk of infringing the regulation enshrined in the EC Schedule of Acceptable Materials for Covering Ceilings. Have a nice Shrove Tuesday.

11

There's nowt so queer as folklore

The marvellous thing about this country is the rich variety of its folklore and customs. The other day I went to one of the traditional springtime celebrations in my area: the Blessing of the Municipal Tip. It takes place on a Sunday morning. All the locals drive up in their cars with the boots stuffed with branches and twigs that they have taken from their garden and junk from their attics. They throw these things into a skip as a sort of offering and also as a symbol that this is a time of renewal.

Meanwhile, the young men of the area, perform a sort of courtship ritual for the young women looking on. They show off their strength by lifting broken pieces of sofas, bedsteads and squirming mattresses and chucking them in the skip. Then, in unison everyone says 'It's a great blessing having a municipal tip' and they drive home again.

A similar sort of ceremony takes place in parts of Norfolk on the second Thursday after Shrove Tuesday. Girls of the town, wearing brightly coloured anoraks, do the Bottle Bank Dance. Holding those fluorescent ribbons that are used to mark off roadworks, they dance round the bottle bank chanting 'Please place all coloured glass in the designated receptacle.' Nobody knows how long this tradition has been going on, but it is clearly associated with nature re-cycling itself as the seasons pass.

On May the 15th every year in the villages of Cheshire people black their faces with charcoal, put on aprons and carry long strings of sausages in and out of all the houses. The woman of every house they visit has to give them a baked potato. This age-old ceremony is designed to appease the gods and to ensure that all the summer's barbecues are successful.

In the evening the oldest inhabitant of the village stands facing the chairman of the Rotary Club. Each one holds a raw lamb chop and ritually slaps the face of the other with it while uttering the words: 'May your briquettes never go out and may your smoke not cause annoyance to your neighbours.'

There is a charming old custom in the Leighton Buzzard area. They say that if a girl gets up before dawn on the second Sunday in May and collects a bag full of those polystyrene worms used for packing and if she then goes and stands outside the DIY Superstore and throws those polystyrene worms over the first man she sees coming out of the store with a can of white emulsion, that is the man she will marry.

In the course of my researches I have discovered many other traditions whose origins are now lost in the mists of time. There is the crowning of the Pick Your Own Raspberries Queen in East Sussex, the annual Festival of Strimmers in Barnstaple and Deep Freeze Open Day in Matlock in Derbyshire when everybody is entitled to go into anybody else's house and inspect the contents of their deep freeze.

Of course, the folk song tradition is as strong as ever. All over Britain in out of the way country pubs never visited by the tourists there are folk karaoke evenings still taking place. There are wonderful old performers like Jethro Gubbins, the singing washing machine service engineer. Jethro's songs celebrate the great stories, the heartbreak and the laughter, of car boot sales of days gone by. One of my favourite songs of his is: 'I got a microwave oven for £1.40, but I lost my one true love.'

Then there are all those marvellous country sayings that you can still hear. Like: 'New Volvo in April; six thousand mile service afore September.' And, of course, the sayings about the weather – 'When John Kettley comes on just before the six o'clock news/A cold wind will blow on your lambs and your ewes.'

12

I forgot Amnesia's real name

Some years ago, the marvellous Katharine Whitehorn included this next piece on absent mindedness in her selection for With Great Pleasure *on Radio 4. I was tremendously flattered and pleased and it must have struck a chord with listeners because many of them remembered to write in and ask for a copy of it.*

In her introductory remarks to the piece, Katharine Whitehorn got me confused with Oliver Postgate and credited me with the creation of the children's TV puppet series, The Clangers. *I didn't mind at all. It was obviously just one of those moments of forgetfulness . . .*

The memory has a brilliant way of cutting out and leaving you in the lurch on social occasions. You arrive at that moment when you cannot avoid introducing your dearest friend to your oldest friend and suddenly life's Teleprompter goes blank. How often do you hide in doorways, or cross the street to escape because a name has escaped you?

Some years ago I had a bad experience collecting my daughter from playgroup. 'And who have you come for?' asked the lady in charge. It was at this moment that all the memory cells decided to stage a spontaneous mass walk-out. I stood there in confusion trying to remember what we had decided to call the child. Amnesia – now *there's* a very nice name for a girl. My raincoat seemed to become shabbier and my fangs began to grow as I desperately scrabbled through a mental list of names. In the end the best reply I could manage was: 'Emily's friend.' That, at least, is something I have never been allowed to forget.

When things get as bad as this you start to take precautions. You leave yourself memos, you scribble essential bits of information, like your own telephone number, on the palm of your hand with a ballpoint pen. You write your wife's name on a piece of paper and put it in your pocket in case of emergency and then when the moment comes you take out the paper and address your wife as Collect Laundry.

A colleague, who is a Catholic, still remembers with head-clutching pain the time he left a cinema in Oxford in the middle of a film. He squeezed along the row of seats past the other members of the audience and then when he reached the centre aisle of the cinema he turned towards the screen and genuflected and made the sign of the cross.

13

Rebels without a clause get all in a huff

There is very real anger in the wolf community over what they consider to be an unwarranted slur by the Prime Minister. Mr Jeremy Lupus, a wolves' spokesman, issued a statement yesterday saying: 'The vast majority of wolves are hard-working and are doing their best to make a worthwhile contribution to society. The last thing we need is to have Little Red Riding Hood thrown in our faces yet again.'

The cause of the resentment is Mr Major's comment that Labour's ditching of Clause 4 was the biggest attempt to con the gullible since the wolf dressed up as Little Red Riding Hood's grandmother.

In an exclusive interview yesterday, Lupus told me: 'This sort of stereotyping is exactly the sort of thing that can lead to an erosion of wolf rights.' He revealed that he was campaigning to have the Red Riding Hood case reopened as there was a mass of new evidence to suggest that the wolf had been the victim of a miscarriage of justice.

I asked him about Mr Major's allegation that the wolf had dressed up in the grandmother's clothes. 'If a wolf wishes to put on women's clothing in private it is surely no one's business but his own,' he replied. 'I certainly would not condemn him. And, in any case, how do we know that this so-called grandmother actually existed? We only have the word of a young woman who is clearly an untrustworthy witness.'

'Untrustworthy?' I asked.

'Why should anyone going about their lawful business in the woods with a basket of groceries feel it is necessary to use an assumed name? Little Red Riding Hood indeed! That is not a name; that is what she wore.'

Lupus said he found it significant that no trace had ever

been found of the horse. 'This red hood she wore was obviously meant for riding. Hence its name. So, if this young woman was dressed for riding, where was the horse? The whole thing stinks. Had she sold the horse to pay for drugs which she was carrying through the woods in a basket disguised as provisions for a totally fictitious grandmother?'

The wolf community is convinced that the whole episode has been used to blacken their name. They think perhaps the young woman posing as Red Riding Hood stumbled across the harmless transvestite wolf and realised that he knew too much and had to be killed.

Questions have been raised about the role of the woodman who was so conveniently nearby and armed with his axe. Was he in on the drugs plot? Was he perhaps the lover of this unidentified young woman who had apparently so conveniently 'mislaid' her horse?

Somehow she managed to convince everybody and place all the blame on a deceased, chopped up wolf. 'The grandmother was invented as a pretext for Little Red Riding Hood to go into the wood that day,' Lupus told me. 'We are being asked to believe that an elderly woman was living on her own in the middle of a wood without the social services knowing about her; it is preposterous.'

Leading wolves are planning to write to the Prime Minister to protest at his weekend remarks and to suggest that he himself has been conned by the powerful Riding Hood lobby who have a vested interest in perpetuating the myth.

A militant wolf organisation, Hands Off Wolf Lifestyle (HOWL), is planning to picket children's bookshops and stage a number of demonstrations around the country, perhaps linking up with anti-foxhunting campaigners.

'We have had enough of being libelled and persecuted,' said Jeremy Lupus. 'My ancestors lived in Russia. They used to run in packs after horse-drawn sleighs, calling out a warning whenever somebody fell off the sleigh, but their efforts were never appreciated.'

In any species, he said, you might get one or two rotten apples, and perhaps sometimes wolves did things that were misunderstood – 'But this is just once in a full moon'.

'What about the allegations concerning a wolf huffing and

33

puffing and threatening to blow down the houses of three little piggies?' I asked fearlessly.

'Those pigs were unscrupulous property developers,' Lupus replied. 'The wolf merely wanted to demonstrate that the houses made of wood and straw were unsound structures. And little thanks he got for it.'

March

14

Weather that is nobler in the mind

After a couple of days, boastfulness creeps in. We begin to indulge in Celsius one-downmanship; we find that we are adopting a more-wind-chilled-than-thou attitude. Out here in my part of the countryside we are proud to announce that Nothing Is Getting Through.

The weather map on television has now become a national scoreboard. I sit here, smugly below zero, jeering at Liverpool, mocking Hull. 'Look, it is almost tropical there,' I scoff. Taking into account the wind chill factor, we are claiming to be something worse than minus sixteen degrees. Beat that, Reykjavik; eat your heart out, Vladivostok. That is the trouble with this sort of weather; it gives you delusions of *froideur*.

In fact, when people complain about the harmful effects of television I am coming to the conclusion that the most corrupting thing to be seen on the box is the weather forecast.

The fake gravity of the weather persons is one of the problems. For all their hand wringing, they are enjoying bringing us the bad news. Deep depressions are meat and drink to them; they are connoisseurs of isobars; what is freezing fog to you is job satisfaction to Ian McCaskill.

But, more importantly, watching these weather forecasts is bad for our character. It divides the nation. East Anglia, in the grip of gales, looks down on the West of England which can only muster some scattered showers; fog-bound Kent sneers at the misty patches of the East Midlands. When Michael Fish says, 'For this bulletin I am going to take all of Southern England together', there are some of us who would rather not be taken together with Sussex, if you don't mind.

Anyway, while sitting contentedly in my own White Hell last week, I was pleased to be able to call out to my wife: 'Our part of the country is bearing the brunt of the bad weather. They have just said so on the TV news.' The news showed pictures of stranded lorries on a white motorway which might have been anywhere, but there is something rather splendid about bearing the brunt.

The dog looks solemn. Every time we let it out into the garden it does an embarrassing impersonation of Captain Oates. Eventually it returns with anxious frosted eyebrows.

Down at the pub, we are waiting to play our competitive games. We do not say much because we are lying in wait for the first innocent fellow who comes through the door, stamps the snow off his feet and says 'Terrible weather. I've never seen anything like it.'

That is our cue. That is when we all say, in unison: 'You obviously weren't here for the Big One of 1987. Now that was really what you call snow.'

The drifts become deeper in the remembering and the stories less plausible – cottages cut off for weeks, huge mansions disappearing completely under snow, convoys of gritting lorries driving off into the blizzard never to be seen again, the thaw revealing a man up a sixty-foot ladder with the hammer still clutched in his hand, the family of fourteen living on one pilchard and half a turnip for a week, and the chap who burned the Chippendale to keep warm.

One thing this weather has shown is that the art of panic buying is in its infancy. While most of us dither round the supermarket shelves of soup and corned beef a flock of hooligan ladies with tartan shopping trolleys swoops down on the bakery department and makes off with all the bread.

The other day a neighbour said he was going to make an attempt to drive into town if he could get up the icy hill. Was there anything I wanted? The car engine was running and there was hardly time to think. I was frozen in indecision. What did I urgently need? A bunch of fresh sage if they had any, a new flannel perhaps, purple preferably, some of the larger sized paperclips, seven second class stamps and a gooseberry yoghurt.

Yes, things are tough here. I am going out now with a lot

of old clothes and tree branches so that I can write a message in the snow in the field opposite to be seen by a passing helicopter. It will say: 'We are bearing the brunt of it.'

15

The queries at the bottom of my garden

Once again nature has performed her annual miracle and 11,533 sycamore seedlings have sprung up overnight on the lawn. We have a forest of five-centimetre-tall sycamore trees. This is how I know that it is the time of year when I have to deal with readers' gardening queries.

Once again, the Post Office has performed its miracle and has delivered 21,533 letters from people pleading for expert advice and tips. Most of these letters have gone straight into my new electric-powered Wunda-Cruncha which chews up everything (including half a wheelbarrow, four dibbers and nine left-hand gardening gloves) and turns it into fine organic compost. I have kept a few back and will deal with them today.

Mrs J.T. of Ipswich writes: 'I am proposing to grow a clematis on my trellis. Am I likely to encounter any problems with this?' The most common problem is one of pronunciation. You have to decide at an early stage whether to say 'clematis' with the emphasis on the first syllable or to pronounce it 'clem-ay-tis' or even 'clem-ah-tis'. If your soil is sufficiently middle-class, I would suggest stress on the first syllable.

Mr C.B. of Sittingbourne asks: 'What would you recommend for a modest back garden measuring about eighteen feet by twelve feet?' The best thing to do is to get a really pretentious pair of wellingtons – 'The Waverley' and 'The Purposeful Strider' are both good varieties with excellent, ingeniously ribbed soles. If you put on these boots and stamp vigorously on the soil you will produce a charming pattern of diamonds and wiggly lines which looks very much like the logo of one of the new privatised water companies or the trade mark of a go-ahead cement manufacturer.

Ms G. de W.-P. writes: 'When is the best time to sow sweet peas, to be sure of success?' Conditions have to be exactly right before you sow sweet peas. I suggest you wait until hell freezes over.

Many people have been asking me to identify the new fashionable trends in horticulture. Undoubtedly, there is an increasing preoccupation with health – and I do not just mean herbs with dubious claims to have curative powers. You will be able to learn more about this when my new book, *Preventive Gardening*, is published later in the year. In the meantime, most good garden centres now sell little notices saying, 'Thank You For Not Growing Tobacco Plants.' These are available in a variety of colours and make an attractive display in herbaceous borders.

This year I am setting aside a small area as an Insomniac's Garden. In it, I am going to plant just night-scented stock, so that if somebody cannot sleep at 2 a.m. she can just go outside and have a sniff. However, she would be well advised, in the darkness, to give the Wunda-Cruncha a wide berth.

Our persistent old friend, the dock plant, raises his ugly head in many of the letters I have received from readers. Once again, I must urge people not to touch this plant. Serious back injury can result from attempts to uproot it. Leave it where it grows and explain to visitors that it is part of the new, organic, pesticide-free garden, as it attracts the Horrid Scabby Mite away from the ornamental gherkins.

Mrs J.P. of Middlesbrough writes: 'Do you have any other clever ideas?' Well, yes I do, actually. Last year my next door neighbour had a very attractive display of antirrhinums. These actually came from seeds I sowed in my own garden on a very windy day. Nothing came up on my side of the fence. But I have held on to fourteen tennis balls that came over from my neighbour's garden. They are the fluffy garishly yellow variety and they make a fine show floating on the surface of my ornamental pond.

I know from your letters that many of you are irritated by the Latin names on the labels of flowering shrubs you buy at nurseries. I just tear off these labels, but leave the price tags. I have planted a pleasing row of shrubs beside my garden path, combining a £14.99 with a £7.33 and a £12.18. Friends gaze at a bush and say 'Good heavens! You mean you paid £15.47 for *that*?'

There has been the usual flood of letters about vegetable gardening. In answer to the perennial question, yes, the rotation of crops *is* important. When your parsnip is well established, grasp it firmly and give it three turns in a clockwise direction. (Leeks should be rotated anti-clockwise.)

Potatoes in the vegetable rack should be well chitted by now and it is time to plant them. 'Earlies' should be planted before 9.15 a.m. and 'lates' put in the ground at least an hour after dusk.

Finally, a timely reminder: British Summer Time began today, so garden sundials should be put forward an hour.

16

Gardening tips

As spring approaches, I am getting thousands of letters from listeners begging for gardening tips. So I thought I would talk today about some of the little jobs you should be doing at this time of the year.

This is the time to get out in the garden and stare glumly at your borders. I like to give a good glum stare all round the borders and maybe even scowl a bit at the rose bushes. If you have honeysuckle this is also a good time to go and mutter threateningly at it.

Go and check over the garden toolshed if you have one. Just give it a few kicks at the base of the wall, if you think it needs it. The wood there should be well rotted now from the winter damp and you should be able to kick quite a good hole in it. The rotted damp wood will have a nice rich crumbly texture when you rub it through your fingers. Garden sheds like to be kicked.

It is also time to look for the gardening gloves. You will probably find that just one of them has survived the winter and the first thing to do is to check whether it is a right hand glove or a left-hand glove. It is quite simple to do this. I'll tell you a little trick. You lay the glove on the ground with the palm facing upwards. Now if the thumb is sticking out to the left it is a left handed glove. That means that you will be gardening left-handed for the rest of the year.

I am often asked about how to feed a lawn. What I do is take a mat from the sitting room and shake it over the grass. You'll find that the mat contains all the nutrients a lawn needs – biscuit crumbs, mineral-rich dog hairs, paperclips and those all-important little balls of fluff. Lawns love those pieces of fluff.

Now it is important to see that these nutrients are pressed well down into the lawn, so jump up and down on it for twenty minutes or so. While you are doing this you could also mutter a few more threats at the honeysuckle. Honeysuckle likes a few blood-curdling threats.

Incidentally, I never use chemical fertilisers in my garden. When the soil needs feeding I pick a wet day and go and walk round my neighbours' garden then come back and scrape their mud off my boots onto my borders. It helps if you have boots with deep-ribbed sole that pick up a lot of this nice rich neighbours' soil.

Here's another handy tip if you need more topsoil. Collect together all your plastic pots with dead dried-up plants in them. You will find that the pots are almost solid with the old roots but there is still some dry dusty soil clinging to those roots. Now, if you throw these pots very hard at the fence this will dislodge the soil and scatter it nice and evenly over your borders.

One feature of my own garden that is much commented-on is the way I have managed to get the water to drip from the broken gutter into an old empty paint tin down below to produce an attractive 'plink' effect all the time. I think it is important to rotate your containers, so that sometimes you have a plastic watering can in place, thus producing a deeper 'plunk' noise. The nice thing about this is that you can get a lovely variety of 'plinks' and 'plunks' all the year round. It is well worth the effort.

Finally this is the time when it is a good idea to thin out your stinging nettles to be sure of a good crop next year. It is really simple; just pull them out quite viciously. One little tip though: remember you have only got a gardening glove on your left hand. If you have overlooked this it may be a good moment now to go and give that old garden shed another kick.

17

The man who bit the bullet in a town called Basics

While rummaging through some old papers in the attic at the weekend I came across some letters and diaries written by my great uncle Eardley when he was in America in the 1870s. As I read them I realised they cast a fascinating light on John Major's connections with that country.

It has been said that the Prime Minister's grandfather Abraham Ball, a master bricklayer, was in Pennsylvania, somewhere near Pittsburgh, building blast furnaces for Andrew Carnegie's steel mills at this time, but little evidence has been found to support the claim.

Now, my discovery of great uncle Eardley's papers over-turns this theory. It seems that one Abraham Ball was a noted figure in the Wild West town of Basics, Wyoming. It was a small lawless place and my great uncle was the barman in the Falling Dollar Saloon. I often think that Eardley must have been the model for the nervous bartender in all those Western films; the one who ducks behind the bar as the cowboys draw their guns.

While crouching on the floor as they smashed the furniture and the bullets shattered the bottles, he would keep his diary up to date and write letters to the family back in South London. I have found a smudged and faded diary entry for what appears to be March 5th 1874. It says: 'Big Jake got shot today over a disagreement about fixed exchange rates. Shortly after sun-up a stranger rode into town. Name of Abe Ball.'

My great uncle's letters show that, after the arrival of that stranger, life was never quite the same in Basics, Wyoming. The first person to notice Abraham Ball was Miss Virginia who used to entertain the men in the Falling Dollar Saloon. She used to sing 'See What the Boys in the Back Room Will

45

Have and Tell them It's Bad for Them.' She took a fancy to Ball right from the start, but he did not respond to her charms because he was too busy. 'I have a very full programme,' he would say.

After the usual Saturday night fight and after the Thatcher Boys, from out of town, had ridden into Basics, whooping and shooting wildly before riding out again, Abe Ball got on a soapbox and addressed the people in the saloon. 'I can negotiate with any man in this bar,' he boasted. He said he was going to clean up the town.

'You haven't got a six-shooter,' my great uncle pointed out.

'No, but I've got a six-point plan,' he replied.

Old Jed Paxman had to give up printing the *Basics Herald Tribune* and all the Wanted posters because he was too busy producing copies of the Cowboys' Charter for Abe Ball. In a letter to the family great uncle Eardley explained the significance of the Charter. 'If I am slow giving a customer his drink or if I don't slide the glass of rye whiskey down the counter just right, instead of hitting me over the head with a chair, the customer can fill in a form and claim compensation. Same thing when the Cheyenne stage-coach comes in late.'

Another provision of the Charter was that no cowboy should be lonesome.

When there was a dispute in the saloon about cheating at poker they would no longer settle it by shooting each other, but the matter would be referred to a conciliation service or to a tribunal or, in the last resort, to an ombudsman.

The next time the Thatcher Boys rode into town they were issued with guidelines telling them not to exceed the speed limit or to allow their horses' hooves to throw up too much dust or to fire their guns after ten o'clock at night.

Inevitably there was a challenge to Abe Ball's authority and this led to the great confrontation which came to be known as the Divergence of Opinion over a Matter of Emphasis at the OK Corral. The Thatcher Boys sent a hired gun to take him on in a duel. Abe's life was saved when the bullet heading for his heart was stopped by the copy of the Cowboys' Charter in his jacket inside pocket.

It was time for Abe Ball to leave. 'My policies on law and order have been a success,' he said, 'and this town is now at ease with itself.' Miss Virginia begged him to stay, but he said 'A man's gotta do what a man's gotta do. Oh yes.' Then he rode off into the sunset, never to return.

I wonder if John Major has ever heard about his grandfather's exploits in Basics. Perhaps he should ask President Clinton to take him back there.

18

A fanfare for the frozen pea

It is amazing that more fuss has not been made of a most important jubilee this year. The frozen pea is fifty years old. Happy Birthday.

You would think, at least, that the Post Office would issue a special 28p stamp to commemorate the launch of the frozen pea in 1938. And where is the in-depth television documentary, paying tribute to its triumph? I hear no fanfare. The Poet Laureate has been strangely silent.

In the absence of any official celebration, I feel it my duty to offer this paean to the frozen pea – so young, fresh and tender and plucked from the pod at dawn, at an hour when the only other people out and about are those who are making television commercials for Hovis or for Milton Keynes.

It would take a keyboard more eloquent than mine to do justice to the colour of the frozen pea. It is a shade of green that can be found nowhere else and one that nature cannot paint. There is a certain luminescence about it, so that it glows in even the most dimly lit and intimate steak houses. It makes the peas easier to find when they slither off the plate on to your lap or the dark red table cloth.

It goes without saying that the invention of the frozen pea was a landmark in the development of convenience food. It is important to remember that word 'convenience' as you wrestle the strong plastic packet with numb fingers before finally tearing it open with your teeth. Then the solid frosty block plops into the pan and you are splashed with scalding water.

One or two peas make their escape at this point, plink on to the floor and roll under the stove where they will turn black and eventually celebrate their own 50th birthdays years hence.

In the deep-freezes of supermarkets, huge packets of frozen

vegetables lie majestically in the mist. They are usually the size of large pillows. Who needs that many frozen peas? There is another mystery about them: the price is a secret. It is seldom, if ever, marked on the packet. At the supermarket check-out the girl has furtively to consult a chart before working out what to charge you.

I have been pondering on how to mark this important anniversary. At the very least the Arts Council should commission a gigantic oil painting by a modern artist using only four colours – tomato ketchup red, frozen pea green, burger brown and fish-finger beige. It could be a mural perhaps, or, if you can bear the pun, a deep frieze.

There must be a gala concert as well, with a performance of Handel's Lightly Salted Boiling Water Music. The National Theatre should be instructed to mount a production of Eugene O'Neill's *The Iceman Cometh* starring John Thaw. I myself am planning a public reading of the poems of Robert Frost.

The occasion could also be marked with a spectacular show on ice, with Torvill and Dean leading a huge cast of skaters dressed as vegetables – peas, French beans, Brussels sprouts, carrots, crinkle-cut chips, cauliflower florets and spinach. The show would reach its climax when the ice melted and all the performers simmered gently for four to six minutes.

If anybody still doubts the significance of this anniversary I would just remind them of Neville Chamberlain's historic and remarkably far-sighted pronouncement fifty years ago that there would be 'Peas in our time'.

19

More suckers hit the road

The link between confectionery and motoring is becoming increasingly important. One of the most significant findings in yesterday's *Daily Telegraph* Gallup survey of motorists was that 27 per cent of them carried boiled sweets in their cars. Disappointingly, it only scratched the surface of this fascinating subject.

It reported, for example, on people's ideas about the characters of drivers of certain types of car – the Porsche man is an aggressive show-off, the person behind the wheel of a Citroen 2CV is Green, and the owner of a Ford Granada is a family man or woman, and so on.

As a result of my own analysis of the contents of glove compartments, I have been able to link particular sweets to the type of car. Thus: BMW–humbug; 2CV–barley sugar; Range Rover–extra strong mints or Fisherman's Friend; VW Golf GTi–Parma violets.

I have been able to give guidance to insurance companies on what combinations of sweets are most likely to lead to accident. Here is one recipe for disaster: a gobstopper tearing along at 65 mph, with a sherbert lemon approaching from a side road and a soft-centre pulling away from the hard shoulder.

Sucking a boiled sweet can give you an accurate notion of time and distance, and this is entering more and more into the language of motorists. People say: 'The traffic was so light that I got to Brighton in seven peardrops' or 'Just carry on along this road for one Glacier mint, then turn left'.

As the percentage of motorists having in-car sweets is likely to increase, the Department of Transport has asked me to report back on the safety aspects.

Some of the most common hazards I have discovered are: (1) sharp fragment of butterscotch caught in throat leading to watering of eyes and impaired vision; (2) lack of care and attention due to driver taking aniseed ball out of mouth to check if it has changed colour; (3) sugared almond spat into face of third party during emphatic altercation at traffic lights.

An accessory that is likely to be seen in next year's models is an automatic sweet unwrapper, taking the place of cigarette lighter on the dashboard. However, this may not be enough to deter the DoT hardliners who are hoping to ban drivers from unwrapping sweets while in motion.

They argue that if people are supposed to stop before they use their car telephones, they ought also to do so to unwrap a sweet. It is pointed out that in hot weather you are likely to need both hands, your teeth and 100 per cent concentration to get the bit of paper off a sticky one.

20

Great trains of thought

A new advertisement for British Rail suggests that you meet some frightfully interesting people when you travel by InterCity. It describes a journey on the 17.30 Pullman from London to Newcastle. Archimedes, toying with the ice in his gin and tonic, makes important observations about the displacement of liquid; Pythagoras discovers his theorem about the square on the hypotenuse, Isambard Kingdom Brunel gets the idea for the Clifton Suspension Bridge and Descartes comes to the triumphant conclusion: 'I think, therefore I travel InterCity'.

Yes, this is all very true to life. In fact, it reminds me of an InterCity journey I made recently. We were scarcely out of Watford when I noticed an earnest man writing furiously in a notebook. My curiosity got the better of me and I fell into conversation with him.

'My name is Dante,' he said, perspiring in the overheated carriage. 'I am just knocking off a great poem about Purgatory. It should be finished by the time we get to Stafford.' I also observed Karl Marx in animated discussion with Engels about the imminent downfall of the Capitalcard system.

The fellow making complicated calculations on the misted-up window turned out to be Euclid. At first I thought he was proving that a railway line was the shortest distance between two points, but it turned out he was just trying to make sense of the British Rail fare structure.

A gang of about a dozen youths kept rushing rowdily up and down the train, pausing occasionally to throw toilet rolls out of the window. 'Just testing the Theory of Relativity,' their leader explained, giving me a thoughtful punch on the nose then running off again chanting 'Einstein is the greatest'.

I was lucky enough to be seated next to the philosopher Bishop Berkeley who was endeavouring to prove that Crewe Junction did not exist. I tried my own little philosophical conundrum on him. 'I wanted to catch the 15.30 InterCity train, but it was cancelled,' I said. 'Can it be said, therefore, that the 15.30 does not exist? After all, an engine and a lot of coaches cannot disappear into thin air. They must be somewhere.'

Berkeley made an excuse and got out at Crewe, stepping out on the wrong side of the train where there was no platform, thereby, in a way, proving his point.

We made an unscheduled stop at Nuneaton. Shakespeare stared out of the window at the W.H. Smith bookstall, jotted down a sonnet and dedicated it to Mr W.H. 'That ought to fox A. L. Rowse,' he said.

The steward announced over the intercom system that no hot beverages were available in the buffet car which was situated towards the centre of the train. All the same I took a stroll along there and I found Alexander Fleming peering at a British Rail sandwich, hoping to discover penicillin. And James Watt was staring glumly at the lifeless tea urn. 'It is a pity it is not working,' he said. 'I might have been able to invent the steam engine.'

April

21

Take a lead from Rover

I was fretting over my tax return the other day when a man came to the door, raised his hat and handed me his business card. His name was Lurcher and he was a financial consultant. He announced that he wanted to offer his services as account- ant and tax adviser to my dog. I said I thought I was the one in need of advice.

Mr Lurcher then produced a copy of George Bush's tax return. It showed that the President's autobiography, *Looking Forward*, had earned him £1,550 last year while *Millie's Story*, an account of life at the top through the eyes of his springer spaniel (ghosted by Barbara Bush) had netted £508,000. He also pointed out that the spy writer Chapman Pincher had registered his labrador Dido as the author of a book entitled *One Dog and her Man*. This, no doubt, was bringing in hand- some royalties.

I suggested to Mr Lurcher that he had only to look at my dog to see that it was not in the high earnings bracket and certainly not in full-time employment. He replied that it could be slipping out regularly to talk to a ghost writer or to earn fees from personal appearances. It could be about to burst into print with sensational 'lick and tell' revelations.

When I came to think of it, I realised the dog did give me pitying looks when I sat down at the keyboard to write, and whenever I threw a stick and shouted 'fetch', its demeanour suggested that I should first discuss the matter with its agent.

All the same, I told Mr Lurcher that I thought I could handle any canine tax matters that might arise. He replied that it was much more complicated. 'You've got to remember that one of our financial years is the equivalent of seven dog financial years,' he said. 'So your dog is already twenty-eight years behind with its tax. It is going to cost you a lot to sort out this mess.'

He said he would help. The dog, he explained, could claim allowances for its offspring, so the more puppies it could produce the better. Then there were the poodle parlour fees it could claim for public appearances and, of course, a certain amount for entertaining foreign breeds.

'Does your dog have any other outgoings?' he asked.

'Well, we usually take it out for a walk twice a day, if that's what you mean,' I replied. He said it might be better in future for the dog to take a taxi if it could be established that it was going out for business purposes.

'Does it have a portfolio?' he asked.

'Just the usual bean-bag,' I replied.

Mr Lurcher explained that sometimes dogs came back home with share certificates which they buried in the garden. He said it was lucky he came round when he did because the tax inspectors in Edinburgh were having a big crackdown at the moment on cocker spaniels like mine. When I confessed to him that the dog was not even registered for VAT he put on a pained expression and gave a low whistle.

Thanks to Mr Lurcher, the whole business has been sorted out. The dog is registered as a limited company with Mr Lurcher as company secretary and myself and my wife as non-executive directors. Now when I take the dog for a walk and old ladies say 'that's a sweet little doggie, what's his name?' I tell them it is called the Consolidated Investment and Development Holdings (Cayman Islands) Corporation.

22

A nice little number in Bradford

There have been criticisms in Bradford of Hockney's depiction of the town hall, the Cow and Calf Rocks and Ilkley Moor on their new local telephone directory. Letters in the local newspaper have called the work 'childish, monstrous and disgraceful'. Those who object to it can simply go ex-directory.

Indeed, if the whole population of Bradford and District took their names and numbers out of the phone book we would be left with nothing but a David Hockney etching.

23

If only I could get a break

It is the gravity of the whole business that makes it so absorbing. Those serious men in waistcoats, the reverent coughing from the audience and the whispered moralising of the commentators all combine to make it addictive.

If ever the revolution comes to Britain the authorities will not need to play solemn martial music over the radio. They can simply put out seventy-two hours of continuous snooker on BBC television. The whole nation will be calmed by watching Ray disturbing a pack of reds, Willie getting a good angle on the green, Steve screwing back and Kirk putting a terrific amount of side on the cue ball.

The unavoidable Embassy World Professional Snooker Championship is here again and I have to confess I am hooked, staring for hours at the screen and that headache-green table, listening to the clink of the cue ball on red and the occasional thuds of the yellow ball into the corner pocket.

It is not the game which is interesting, but the ceremonial. There is that severe man in white gloves who appears to be trying to strangle the black ball before he puts it back on its spot. There is the pleasure of speculation, too. Have you noticed that the match at the next (unseen) table always seems more exciting? While you are watching Joe playing his nineteenth safety shot, there is suddenly an explosion of applause from the other match. Has Kirk got nicely on to the blue or has Jimmy got a fine cut on the pink? Terry sits deadpan while his opponent clears the table. Is he still brooding about the difficult red he missed?

The commentators are marvellous. One of them affects a John Arlott growl and has a tendency to portentousness. The other suffers from bouts of pessimism.

They are like two men leaning over your garden fence telling you your guttering is about to fall down, or looking into your car engine and not holding out much hope for your carburettor.

'That leaves Willie needing snookers,' they say. 'Steve is a bit unfortunate to have landed there,' they murmur. 'Joe won't be happy with that shot,' they lament. 'That is not the angle Kirk would have liked,' they mourn. Every so often Willie or Kirk or Steve or Joe will stand beside the table looking remarkably serene considering that they are working out the next seventeen shots of the break and the commentary box Jeremiahs will declare that they are 'under pressure'.

It is an allegory of course. That is the excuse for watching. Don't you find that, in life, you always seem to require eighty-eight points when there are only a possible fifty-nine points left on the table? We all have that feeling when we wake up in the morning that we require snookers if we are to survive the frame of life.

Every day we discover we have left ourselves in an unfortunate position: we are not happy with the angle and the only thing to do is to go for safety. When we are under pressure the pink always seems to teeter on the brink of the top right-hand corner pocket and refuses to go in. Why does the other chap always seem to get the big breaks while we sit it out and brood? There could be a sermon in all this.

Meanwhile I spend the evenings slumped on the sofa watching this lesson in life from the Crucible Theatre in Sheffield, with a bottle of claret to help me survive the pressure. The hours pass and I steadily sink the red. As midnight approaches I find myself, as they say, tight against the cushion.

24

How to wake up without any alarm

The Prime Minister, it said in the paper, was woken at 5 a.m. to be told the news. I have always been fascinated by reports of world leaders having their slumbers disturbed to be informed of coups, typhoons and other upheavals. Actually, it is a job I have always rather hankered after.

I think I would be good at it. Over the years one learns to develop an early-morning bedside manner. It is important not to be too hearty – not too much of that 'wakey, wakey, rise and shine' stuff, which can make you a bitter enemy for life. At the same time, you cannot be too cooingly tactful or your victim will nod off again and blame you later.

There is the problem of shaking the shoulder. You tiptoe to the bed, all concern and sympathy, reach out, grip the shoulder and gently rock it back and forth. In a split second you have a starring part in this person's nightmare; you are the leering, one-eyed, chasm-mouthed monster who has been chasing them down a long, long corridor lined with filing cabinets in the basement of their old school.

You get a nasty shock when they shriek and leap two feet into the air. They give you a look of terror and loathing that slowly turns to recognition and resentment. Meanwhile, you are clinging to the chest of drawers, trying to control the pounding of your heart. You are also offended. 'So, there we have it,' you say bitterly. 'That is what your subconscious really thinks of me.' The atmosphere is soured for a while.

Obviously, this would be no way for a Prime Minister to start a day of international crisis when there are statements to be made, messages of support to be sent and telephone conversations with President Bush to be conducted – 'I had this awful dream, George. I was . . .'

As an alternative to the shake of the shoulder I have some-times tried the tug of the big toe. This can be effective, but there is a risk of being kicked in the solar plexus if the person is having one of those anxiety dreams about running over shingle to catch a train.

Tact is the watchword. You do not march cheerily into the bedroom saying, 'If it's Tuesday, it must be the dentist at 2.45.' And you do not chuck the letters on to the bed saying, 'Your bank has written to you again.'

A small lie is permissible. I sometimes look out of the window and say: 'Ah, sweet! A humming-bird is hovering over the lilies in the fishpond, a kingfisher is perched on the telephone wire and a baby deer is sipping the dew from the petals of that yellow rose.' This will help the subject wake up in a reasonably good mood.

I am sure that readers are all bursting to know how I would have handled the crisis of the coup in the Soviet Union if I had been the Official Rouser at 10 Downing Street.

Obviously, in my little cubby hole near the Prime Minister's bedroom I would have a booklet listing Reasons for Disturbing the Prime Minister. These reasons would also be graded according to urgency. It would say, for example, 'Victory for British women's 4 × 100m relay team in Tokyo athletics com-petition – any time after 6 a.m.'; or 'Resignation of Dutch Finance Minister – not before 8.30 a.m.'

Having established that the overthrow of Mr Gorbachev qualified as a 5 a.m. job, I would still remain absolutely calm. I would not hammer on the bedroom door shouting, 'Quick, Prime Minister! All hell has been let loose!' This might easily lead him to believe that a fault had developed in the Exchange Rate Mechanism.

I would break it gently. I would make a cup of tea and, adopting a Jeevesian air, enter the bedroom, taking care not to trip over the red ministerial boxes scattered over the floor.

'Good morning, Prime Minister,' I would say.

A noise would come from the sleeping figure in the bed. 'Not an inconsiderable *snrrgghlehmm.*'

I would go to the window and draw back the curtains. 'Well, they've certainly got a nice day for it,' I would say.

'For what?'

'For their coup. Those conservative hardliners.'

By this time Mr Major might well be up. Up somewhere near the ceiling. I would have to explain that I meant the conservative hardliners in the Kremlin, not the ones rather nearer to home. He would still be a bit shaken so I would look out of the window and say, 'Ahhhh. There's a lamb gambolling in Downing Street. It is wearing a garland of daisies and a humming-bird is hovering over its head. And there is a wren feeding her babies on the windowsill. Ah, sweet!'

25

Red sky in the morning, election warning

Predicting the date of a general election can be rather like forecasting the weather: the traditional, folkloric, country ways are often more accurate than the clever scientific approach. Rooks nesting in May blossom or cows lying down on damp seaweed are a sure sign that the weather is going to be changeable and uncertain and are probably a better guide than any study of isobars, low pressure areas or satellite pictures.

As there has been so much speculation lately about the date of the next General Election, I decided to go and see the old boy in our village who knows about these things. He is Seth the Psephologist and he lives in a dilapidated cottage on the edge of the meadow down by Middle Ground. It is said round these parts that he correctly predicted the date of the 1979 election by throwing a dead stoat at a calendar and seeing where it landed. He revealed the date of polling day a whole fortnight before it actually occurred.

I found him sitting on the fence carving a long piece of wood with his penknife. 'Is that a swingometer you've got there?' I asked.

'Of course it aint, you daft old Liberal,' the grizzled psephologist replied. ''Tis a random sampler. You use this in your opinion polling to get your random sample. Anybody knows that.'

'Is there going to be an election soon?' I asked.

Old Seth looked up at the sky, narrowed his eyes, sniffed and spat. Then he said: 'When Gallup and Mori do both agree/T'will be third Thursday in June, just you see.'

'That is very helpful,' I said.

Old Seth wagged his bony finger in my face and warned:

'But if NOP is the same as Mori/Vote afore Lammas, or you'll be sorry.'

With his two fox terriers, named David and Jonathan Dimbleby, barking at his heels, Seth led me into his low ceilinged cottage and poured me a glass of his oilseed rape homemade wine. I admired some of the ancient psephology implements hanging on the wall – a minor party squeezer, a hustings prod, a thatched clipboard and a fiercesome mantrap designed to catch the unwary canvasser in its powerful jaws.

I mentioned that it was good to see that the weather was getting milder after that nasty cold spell. 'Oh yes,' old Seth replied, gazing out of the window. 'That John Cole won't be needing his old overcoat for much longer now. And it wouldn't surprise me to see the first signs of the manifestos popping up soon. They do say, when the manifestos are out, polling day can't be far behind.'

'I suppose the Government will need to feel that the economy is coming right first,' I suggested. 'Do you have an excruciating rhyme for this scenario?'

'Till interest rates do start to come down/In Tory marginals they'll wear a frown,' old Seth replied gloomily.

He mentioned some other telltale signs that would suggest an imminent election campaign – the early sprouting of television cameras and crews in Downing Street, increased activity in advertising agencies, Norman Lamont smiling more often, Chris Patten getting his hair cut and the Prime Minister appearing on the Jimmy Young programme.

'There's an old saying among broadcasting folk and studio technicians,' the wise psephologist remarked. 'They say that when the Prime Minister appears on Radio 2 there'll soon be plenty of overtime on *Panorama*,' he cackled and wheezed. 'They also say it's better to be a pundit than a candidate. Them as don't hand in their nomination papers can't lose their deposits.'

26

A table in the name of King Arthur

Ever since the serpent said to Eve: 'No, really, I insist, the fruit is on me; I can charge it,' the expense account lunch has been a fundamental part of our existence.

It was particularly painful for me to read last week that Mr Edward Booth-Clibborn had lost his job as chairman of the Designers and Art Directors Association of London after he had claimed £448.10 for a meal for two at Le Gavroche. All the same, I am confident that the ancient institution of the business lunch will survive this setback and that it will remain at the heart of our national life.

Over the past few days I have been lunching about town, picking up the bills and the odd nugget of information along the way, so that I could prepare this essay.

Who could quibble at the bill for £322.75 at L'Addition Outrageuse, a little place I know in Fulham, for this historical scoop? Everybody is familiar with the date 1066, but until now nobody has understood its full significance. It was in 1066, shortly after the Battle of Hastings, that King William had lunch with some business associates at a wine bar in St Leonards – 're possible future projects', as he put it in a note to his accountant.

The meal had been going on for some time and they had moved on to liqueurs and the waitress was anxious for them to settle up when William realised that not much business had been discussed. 'Anybody got any ideas for future projects?' he said, after tapping his knife against a glass to catch their attention.

One of his executives, Gerard de Gourmandise, who had become sentimental by this time, said: 'We ought to design a tie. There ought to be a special tie for all the chaps who were

67

there at the Battle of Hastings and flogged their guts out to make it the bloody marvellous success it was.'

There was a general growl of approval round the table and King William said: 'I like the sound of it, Gerard. Let's fix up a lunch and discuss it in more depth.' That is how the Bayeux Tapestry was born.

Later last week, over the £188 set menu for two at the new Chinese restaurant the Dragon and Platinum Credit Card, I gathered another snippet. It was at a lunch in Runnymede that some barons got together and started grousing about King John. There were the predictable complaints – refusal to delegate, failure of baron-to-king communication, lack of co-ordination, no clear leadership on goals, etc. They jotted down their complaints on the back of a menu and, emboldened by another expensive bottle of the Château Lafite (1202, very good year), decided to march in and just tell him.

As it turned out, King John was entirely amiable and agreed with good grace to the demands about the rights of the Church and feudal customs and so on. The only sticking point was the lunch bill the barons submitted. 'I'll sign the Magna Carta, but not this bill,' the King said. The barons had to do rather a lot of negotiating before he consented.

Another wonderful thing the business lunch has given us is the working breakfast. The concept of the working breakfast was first dreamed up over lunch by Cyril Moody and Jefferson T. Snelgrove at Ma Fraser's chop house in Baltimore on March 17, 1922. They hit on the idea while going through their diaries and failing to find a mutually convenient date for a further meeting. The bill from that historic luncheon is now displayed in the Living Museum of Executive Hospitality in St Louis, Missouri.

27

Did Goliath sling the match and make a giant blunder?

The world of sling-shot was rocked yesterday by allegations that an important match was fixed in advance. In the historic encounter between David and Goliath in the Valley of Elah, Goliath, it was claimed, was paid to 'throw' the contest.

At the time, the burly philistine was hot favourite to win against the relatively unknown son of Jesse. The actual result was regarded as one of the Old Testament's biggest sporting upsets. It also put an end to Goliath's unbeaten record.

The National Sling-shot Association (NSSA) has instituted an urgent inquiry and called on anybody with information to come forward and give evidence. It hopes also to interview a number of philistines. 'If there is anything behind these allegations it will be an absolute tragedy for the game,' an NSSA spokesman said.

'It also sets a very bad example to the average young shepherd boy who likes to go out at the weekend with his sling and five smooth pebbles.'

There were calls for the sling-shot authorities to root out corruption and clean up their act. 'It's a bad day when sleaze enters the very heart of our national sport,' said a member of the all-party backbench Slings and Staves Committee.

Meanwhile, a spokesman for the Association of Suppliers of Smooth Pebbles accused some sections of the media of over-reacting to allegations as yet unproved. 'It is wrong to put all the blame on the slingers,' he said. 'After all, the world of sling-shot only reflects what goes on in the rest of society.'

Critics are arguing that there is too much money at stake in the game, that the suppliers of pebbles, the makers of the slings and of the 'scrips' (the bags in which the pebbles are carried) can earn a very good living.

The rewards for smiting philistines are higher than ever. A top smiter, or a slinger with a good aim, can expect to earn fabulous sums from sponsorship and endorsements. After his victory over Goliath, David has certainly not looked back.

Last night he was refusing to comment on the latest allegations, and his representatives were pointing out that he had not actually been accused of anything. However, eyebrows were certainly raised at the time of his victory. He had, after all, come from nowhere, and his opponent, Goliath, the man from Gath, was six cubits and a span in height. It was generally agreed that the other men in the army of Israel were dismayed and sore afraid.

One leading sling-shot commentator said: 'I was frankly amazed that the authorities allowed the bout to go ahead in the first place. Here you had a young lad taking on a bloke with a helmet of brass upon his head, with the weight of his coat of mail being 5,000 shekels of brass.

'I mean, you're looking at somebody the staff of whose spear was like a weaver's beam, while the head of that spear weighed 600 shekels of iron. Not forgetting that one bearing a shield went before him.'

It is now being suggested that a syndicate of philistines were betting heavily on a David victory at very long odds. Goliath himself was making confident pre-fight predictions, saying that he would give David's flesh to the fowls of the air and the beasts of the field. Was this just an act, put on for the benefit of onlookers and the officials refereeing the fight?

It later emerged that, while guarding his father's sheep, David had already smitten and slain a lion and a bear, but these feats had not been achieved under official NSSA rules and would not therefore have been registered.

Questions are being asked about how a pebble could smite the forehead of an experienced warrior wearing a helmet of brass. If Goliath 'took a dive' for the benefit of the philistine betting syndicate it did not do him any good, because David then took his sword and cut off his head. Was this part of a pre-arranged plan?

Perhaps David was actually in league with the philistine syndicate and cut off Goliath's head to stop him selling his story to the second book of Samuel. There are also doubts about the role of Saul in all this. There were subsequent Old Testament reports of Saul falling out with David. Perhaps it was a dispute about his percentage. The truth may never come out.

All we can say is that this episode has been a severe blow to the world of slinging as we know it.

May

28

How to gather nuts in May

Once again there is reckless talk about abolishing the May Day Bank Holiday. People who propose this do not realise how many of our country's precious traditions they would be destroying. They should understand there is more to it than the nostalgia of Tony Benn addressing a workers' rally and the St John's Ambulance Brigade unwinding people from maypoles.

Yesterday, in my own neighbourhood, we observed the age-old custom of crowning the bottle bank queen. This was followed by the blessing of the car wash and then we went on to the opening of some 1992 home brewed beer.

In parts of Lincolnshire, they still observe the rite of 'blerriking' – that is, taking out the village scold, chasing her down the street and bombarding her with barbecue briquettes. This is usually taken in good part and most of the subsequent legal actions are settled out of court.

P. W. Naismith, in his book *Ancient Lore of the M25 and Its Surroundings* records that, on the first Monday in May, people near Junction 19 get together and cook an enormous boil-in-the-bag cod in parsley sauce on the village square.

I could cite thousands of examples of May Day traditions that would be threatened if the bank holiday abolitionists had their way. There is first footing at the garden centre in Solihull, where a man with a handful of potting compost steps over the threshold as a way of ensuring that all cuttings do well in the coming year.

In Fittleworth in Sussex, maidens gather in the fields and put garlands of bright yellow oilseed rape flower in their hair and then go from house to house, where the occupants hand over their credit cards to them. In parts of Suffolk, people beat their neighbours with holly branches while accusing them of not returning the lawn mower they borrowed last summer.

Dr Patricia Fright, in her authoritative work *Nowt So Queer As Folk Lore* (Saskatchewan University Press), has put forward the theory that the military parades that used to take place in Moscow were, in fact, based on ancient customs still to be found in half a dozen villages in Cheshire. In these places, the whole population turns out on the Monday and parades down the main street pushing wheelie bins and baby buggies while the top brass of the local neighbourhood watch take the salute. You can work out the watch's pecking order by seeing where they stand on the balcony of the public library.

Some of the most colourful celebrations take place in the office of the BBC Travel Unit. The room is decorated with luminous orange tape, motorway cones and various roadsigns that have been looted on the travel unit 'rag day' and everybody is in a festive mood.

Every time someone reports a tailback of more than four miles he or she has to sink a yard of ale and swallow three hard boiled eggs. They make music by beating hubcaps and sing the ballads that have been sung on the hard shoulder for generations. They dance the jigs their forefathers used to dance in the service areas in days gone by. Then they get in a line like people doing a conga and perform 'the contraflow' going up and down the stairs, weaving in and out the studios of Broadcasting House. Could anyone really want to abolish the Bank Holiday and put this wonderful heritage at risk?

29

Enough is enough

We are being rather fobbed off and humoured by those people in Brussels who are allowing us to keep our pint and our mile when the great fog of metrication descends on us. The truth is that our hostility to kilos and grammes and metres and all that is not due to some churlish chauvinism, but to the fact that the metric system is just not a very good one.

I propose a much more useful scale of measurement: two *smidgins* make one *teensy bit*; four *teensy bits* equal one *soupçon*; there are six *soupçons* in a *dash* and 22 *dashes* in a *dollop* and 100 *dollops* make *a fair bit*. There are seven *fair bits* in a *say when*.

What has the metric system ever done for us? It has given us the millimetre which is just a blur on a ruler. It has given us the tape measure with centimetres on one side and inches on the other.

I have not dared to go near a swimming pool since I started worrying that they might be marking the depths of the water in metres. A person could easily drown while trying to multiply some figure by 3.28084 in his head. It would be clearer if they indicated the depths with notices like 'Alexander would be in difficulties' or 'That's far enough, Jemima!'

Not that the old Imperial system is much better. The units are so difficult to visualise. When a chap tells me he has caught a seven pound mullet I have to dash out and buy a quarter of dolly mixtures, weigh the bag in my hand and try to get the idea of 28 bags.

When I read that a certain place is 3,000 ft above sea level I have to imagine 500 friends who are six feet tall, assemble them on a beach and mentally stack them one on top of the other. At this point I realise that I don't have 500 friends, even if I bend the rules and include shorter people. Then depression sets in.

I am not all that enamoured of the mile either, as I struggle in my head to straighten out an athletics circuit and multiply it by four. A mile is also a very variable unit of measurement. Miles in country lanes are much longer than those in cities. The sign post, with wild optimism, says that it is only four miles to the picturesque unspoiled hamlet of Nether Ridley and two hours later you still have not even reached the outskirts.

Another baffling unit of measurement is a furlong. The only way I can explain it is to say that the final furlong in a horse race is when the commentator's voice goes up an octave.

Anyway, when the race is over the commentator announces that such-and-such a horse has won by a nose. I have searched through the weights and measures conversion tables at the front of my Pushy Young Executive's Diary and there is no information in it about how many noses there are in a short head, how many short heads in a neck, how many necks in a length and how many lengths in a furlong.

I do, finally, have one simple trick for converting acres into hectares. Take one 20-acre field, plough it up and plant barley. The acres are immediately converted in hectares, producing 'tonnes' of barley for the grain mountain. That's the only language they understand in Brussels.

30

On the seventh day he lagged the boiler

I was in the front garden the other morning, Hoovering the hydrangea, when I saw Mr Devenish coming down the street. Of course, I dropped everything, ran inside and hid in the airing cupboard. I waited for three minutes and forty-four seconds after he knocked on the front door, then I thought it was safe to come out and peep through the upstairs window.

There he was smiling benignly up at me. I had to go down and let him in. 'Sorry, I was reading a book or something,' I mumbled.

It is ridiculous. Why does Mr Devenish always make me feel so guilty? He is the manager of the local do-it-yourself megastore, Do-Rite, which stocks everything for the home-improver. He is a perfectly nice chap, but you can never really relax in his company.

After a certain amount of the usual small talk about things like original sin, the Renaissance and Africa, he got round to what I knew was bound to come up. He gave a little cough and said: 'I am sorry that I have not seen you in the DIY megastore on a Sunday recently.'

'Well, you know I'm not much of a one for that sort of thing,' I said, stuffing the dog's bone under the armchair cushion.

He just looked at me with that infuriating tolerant smile and said nothing. 'Of course, my wife is quite a regular attender,' I went on. 'Only a couple of Sundays ago she was at your place buying a louvre door and a power drill.'

'Ah yes, the wives. Bless 'em,' he sighed. 'What would we do without them? Still, you really ought to think about popping along. The piped music is really very good. The parking facilities are excellent and on Sunday it's very much an occasion for all the family. Since the Court of Appeal

79

judgment on Sunday trading, we are hoping for a good turn-out.'

'It's just that I'm rather busy on a Sunday,' I said, standing by the window to block his view of the sagging sash-cord. 'You know, preparing the lunch, scraping the odd potato.'

'A wise old ceramic-tile grouter once said something to me that I'll always remember,' Mr Devenish said. 'He told me never to ignore the important details in life. What is the point of being the best cook in the whole world if the edges of your pine kitchen unit are not flush?' I told him I would try to do better and showed him out, hoping he did not notice how the front door was sticking because of warping.

'Now, remember,' Mr Devenish said, 'the Do-Rite DIY megastore is not just for people who have made good all their surfaces; it is also there to help those who wish to improve.'

The worst thing is when he comes into the pub. You could cut the atmosphere with a Stanley knife. Of course, he tries to be hearty and wants everybody to call him Doug, but it just doesn't work somehow. 'Don't worry,' he says. 'I'm not going to ram chipboard and aluminium step-ladders down your throat.'

We all sit there awkwardly, horribly aware that the legs of the pub tables are uneven and the pointing in the brickwork round the fireplace is not all it might be. Some people look at the sticking-plaster on their chiselling wounds and feel furtive and rub fretfully at the spots of emulsion paint on their ties.

To be quite honest – though I would never dare mention it to Mr Devenish – the reason I don't attend the Do-Rite DIY megastore these days is that I can't stand it now that they have messed about with the measurements. All these metres and centimetres and litres! I mean, it is just not the same without the mystery and poetry of feet and inches and pints. And this paying with credit cards is supposed to make DIY more 'accessible', but a lot has been lost in the process. There was something to be said for the ritual of going to the ironmonger and getting a dozen six-inch nails wrapped in a bit of brown paper.

Nowadays, you get Mr Devenish standing at the exit shaking hands with all the customers as they come out. If it goes on like this you'll be expected to skip about and make a 'sign of peace' every time you buy a can of wood preserver. The other thing that gets on my nerves is their ghastly handier-than-thou attitude at the DIY megastore on a Sunday.

I rather suspect that Do-Rite is becoming rather 'evangelical'. Mr Devenish is targeting people who attend the garden centre. He is suggesting that they are in danger of being cast into outer darkness because they will be unable to avail themselves of the unbeatable value of his special offer on extension leads.

31

Lord of the aisles by royal appointment

Those of us who live in the fast lane (i.e. the cash-only quick checkout queue in the supermarket) are delighted to hear that the Prince of Wales is selling free-range lamb to Tesco. We feel that the royal connection must surely stimulate interest in the sadly neglected subject of supermarket etiquette.

The thought that, as you take the sharp bend with your trolley at the end of the jams and preserves aisle, you might come face to face with a member of the Royal Family carrying the gold ceremonial price-labelling gun will surely raise standards of behaviour.

The royal free-range lamb (packed in green biodegradable trays, stamped with the Duchy of Cornwall crest) will, to start with, go on sale only in Tesco stores in Truro, Cornwall, and Sandhurst, Berkshire, but the scheme is bound to be extended. Sales of Highgrove Organic Loaves to the same supermarket chain have been a great success.

I have always felt that a person who pushes his trolley anti-clockwise and against the tide in a supermarket should be hounded out of society and forced to live in some distant malarial part of the colonies, and that the bounder who tries to sneak seven items through the 'five items or less' check-out should be struck off all invitation lists. Now, with royal patronage, we may perhaps expect some of these sanctions to be applied.

The rules of etiquette will be formalised. It will be possible to settle once and for all the vexed question of who takes precedence at the delicatessen counter. Is it the person wanting the taramasalata, or the couple queuing for the dolcelatte? Can a customer with a vegetable samosa pull rank on the chap with the Scotch egg?

The lady without scruples who parks her trolley to save her place at the check-out and then scurries off all over the place, fetching a jelly here and a jumbo-sized pack of disposable nappies there, will feel the full weight of social disapproval.

Not only will she have to endure the haughty, withering glare of the Lady of the Cashtill, but she may find that she is no longer admitted to the Frozen Vegetable Enclosure in Special Offer Week.

A visit to Tesco will now become an uplifting experience. As you make your way down the aisle past the magnificent ranks of processed peas, all stacked in dead straight lines, you think to yourself, 'Ah yes, this is the sort of thing the British do best.'

Your way is blocked by two ladies who have parked their trolleys broadside on and are deeply engaged in a conversation which is probably all about the glittering charity ball held by Lady Safeway last night.

You give a deep bow and say: 'I wonder if I might trouble you to pass me a tin of baked beans, as blessed by the private chaplain of the Earl of Hounslow?'

'La, sir,' one of the ladies replies with a coquettish curtsy, 'I suppose you will be eating them with the low-fat pork sausages autographed by the Marquess of Newport Pagnell and some mashed organic potatoes as grown in the chemical-free soil of the estates of the Duke of Waitrose.'

After joining the crowds enjoying all the pageantry of the ceremony of the Slicing of the Corned Beef, you summon one of the Tesco flunkies. 'Tell me, my good man,' you say, 'Where do I find the instant blancmange mix which is free of artificial colouring and the Duchy of Cornwall wholemeal alphabet spaghetti in italic lettering?'

The flunky points to a distant row of shelves. 'It is down there,' he says. 'Between the Honi Soit Quiche and the Mal y Scones.'

32

Bard of the Yard

The news this week that an anthology of poems by police officers is likely to be published next year comes as no surprise to scholars. The police, after all, have made a most important contribution to British poetry.

Every schoolboy knows the line from P-c Shelley's 'Ode to a Skylark' ''Ello, 'ello, 'ello blithe spirit.'

Then there is Constable Gray's 'Elegy at Lighting Up Time in a Country Churchyard' written in his notebook while he was keeping a ploughman under observation.

And who could fail to thrill to the lines of P-c Blake of CID:

> Tiger! Tiger! Burning bright
> With defective near-side light.

Besides being one of the Yard's most successful thief-catchers, Detective Inspector 'Willie' Wordsworth used to turn his hand to poetry in idle moments before a dawn swoop.

His description of daffodils in Hyde Park is still widely quoted in E Division.

> I proceeded westerly as a cloud
> That floats on high o'er vales and hills,
> When all at once I saw a crowd,
> An unlawful assembly of daffodils;
> Beside the lake, beneath the trees,
> In a manner likely to cause a breach of the peace.

Although some of the traditionalists in the Force criticised Wordsworth's unorthodox methods, his metre and his rhymes, he always remained popular with the man on the beat.

Crime-buster Coleridge, of the Drugs Squad, made himself a legend in the Met for his daring Kubla Khan Caper, but he, too, was not averse to a bit of versifying in the canteen during off-duty hours.

His most famous epic is the one about the Ancient Mariner who caused an obstruction on the footpath after a wedding to the annoyance of passers-by and when cautioned made a statement which went on for about a hundred verses. Although Coleridge used up several notebooks in the process he succeeded in getting the Mariner to confess to the unlawful slaying of a sea bird, namely an albatross.

They still joke down at the Leman Street nick about PC Keats who had a habit of bursting into verse when making arrests. Their favourite is:

> O what can ail thee Knight at Arms
> Who with intent art loitering?

Police forces patrolling the South Coast also have their share of Bards in Blue. Detective Constable 'Nipper' Masefield is known to the general public for the time he boarded a ship and discovered a quantity of Quinquireme of Nineveh from distant Ophir and other suspicious substances, but he put pen to paper from time to time.

His superiors were particularly impressed by his report:

> Dirty British coaster with a cargo of immigrants.
> Butting through the Channel in the mad March days.

What is fascinating about police poetry is that it extends to all ranks of the force. Commissioner 'Bill' Shakespeare, of course, used to lend a hand with the theatrical festivities, but he was also widely reported to have a few sonnets tucked away in the bottom drawer of his desk.

He used to strike terror in the hearts of villains with his couplet:

> Shall I compare thee to the Brothers Kray?
> Thou art more lovely and more temperate.

Commenting on the progress of the anthology a Scotland Yard spokesman said this morning: 'We are anxious to interview a Muse who we believe may be able to assist us.'

The police say they have information to suggest that the Muse could be a female. Members of the public are urged not to approach her or to 'have a go' at writing poetry, as this could be dangerous.

33

English poetry in motion

The influence of the commuting tradition on British poetry has not been sufficiently acknowledged. Those evocative words 'British Rail regrets . . .' are clearly part of the first line of some poignant sonnet which I am surprised not to find in the *Dictionary of Quotations*. And the loudspeaker announcements about 'The front four carriages furthest from the ticket "barrier" have such ingenious alliteration and such a catchy metre that they could only be an extract from an epic poem.

All commuters are poets. Every day they come in the rush hour to London's termini – bards from Bexleyheath, versifiers from Virginia Water, lyricists from Lewisham, rhymsters from Rochester and the laureates of Luton.

Today and tomorrow some thirty-six poets will be performing on the concourse at Waterloo Station as part of some event called Poetry Live, which got under way yesterday. They include Benjamin Zephaniah, the Rastafarian who just missed becoming a visiting fellow at Trinity College, Cambridge, someone referred to as 'a screeching punk poetess' and another who is 'the enfant terrible of the gay community'. I am afraid this is a pointless exercise as they will all be outshone by the commuters alighting from their trains.

The poetic tradition of the rush hour goes back a very long way. Indeed there is even a reference to commuting in that famous line from Ecclesiastes: 'To every place there is a season ticket and a timetable to every station.'

Back in the thirteenth century the eventual arrival of a train which had been held up by frozen points outside Dartford was celebrated with the lines:

The 7.15 is icumen in
Lhude sing hooray.

Scholars believe that Shakespeare himself experienced the frustrations of signal failures between Stratford-on-Avon and London. They cite his line in the sonnet: 'Shall I compare thee to an unavoidable delay?'

Shelley, too, experienced the overcrowded platforms and the hectic scramble for seats on Network South East: 'Oh wild West Norwood, thou breath of autumn's being.' He was inclined to strike up conversations in the compartment with other commuters. One such conversation is recorded in the line: 'My name is Ozymandias, I come from Tring.'

Tennyson wrote much of his poetry while travelling in the rush hour and used to become very tetchy when the loud conversation of his fellow commuters interrupted his Muse. Sometimes he would officiously summon a railway employee with the words: 'When do we come into Morden, guard?'

Interestingly, Tennyson refers to the suburban station, Shalott, which was subsequently closed during the Beeching reorganisation of the railways.

This charming station is commemorated in the lines:

'The curse is come upon me,
The refreshment car is shut' cried
The Lady of Shalott.

When you are crammed into a commuter train which is stuck outside Sidcup or when you gaze wanly at the list of cancellations it is comforting to know that some of our greatest poets shared these experiences and found inspiration in them for some of their most famous lines.

34

The lost sport of winning gracefully

Sporting Authorities are still divided as to what is the proper method of punching the air in victory. There are many who favour the gesture that begins just below knee level and looks as if you are delivering a fierce uppercut to the jaw of an invisible adversary who is only three feet tall. This is what the purists say is the correct technique.

Others insist that it should be an overarm gesture – a sort of custard pie throwing motion without the custard pie. And there is still a strong body of opinion that favours a limp version of the Black Power salute.

Certain extrovert footballers believe that the way to celebrate scoring a goal is to stand in front of a section of their supporters, bend their arms and their knees and do a mime of lifting a three-ton slab of concrete – with the appropriate facial contortions showing a combination of ecstasy and excruciating pain.

It is to be hoped that the sporting bodies will get together soon to lay down rules to standardise air-punching. The urgent need for such a move was brought home last Saturday after the Boat Race when the successful Oxford crew engaged in boorish triumphalism, gloating and unseemly gesticulating.

Quite obviously, the poor innocent lads were at a loss as to how to behave in victory. It was a moment of social awkwardness which might have been overcome if somebody had had the presence of mind to hand the crew a jeroboam of champagne which they could shake vigorously and squirt all over each other and into the eye of the race umpire.

Not all that long ago, sportsmen could emulate actors at a curtain call in their displays of agonised false modesty.

The rugby player who scored a try managed to look as if

he was so embarrassed he wished the ground would swallow him up; the cricketer who scored a century would hang his head in shame at such exhibitionism and the tennis player who won the Singles Final could manage to look as if he did not even know what the score was.

Things are much more difficult these days. In tennis, the victor cannot get away with a diffident handshake; he must hurl his racket into the sky, fling himself on to his knees and punch the air. All this requires a considerable feat of co-ordination and makes vaulting the net look rather churlishly undemonstrative.

It is, in fact, the anxiety about throwing my racket in the air and hitting a spectator on the forehead that has always put me off entering the Men's Singles at Wimbledon. Similarly, although I can see no problem in the footballing aspects of leading my team to triumph at Wembley, I am not altogether confident of my technique in actually kissing the FA Cup and holding it aloft without dropping it.

Punching the air is not just for sportsmen. It is an all-purpose celebration of success. Accountants do it when the figures add up; others do it when they get a mortgage or complete the *Telegraph* Crossword. I have seen people do it when their home-made mayonnaise does not curdle. No doubt micro-surgeons punch the air when they finish their last micro-stitch.

All this shows how important it is to formalise the gesture and to settle authoritatively the great underarm/overarm controversy. That is why I am campaigning to have punching the air made an official competitive event at the Olympic Games. People could be awarded points for technique and presentation. I wonder what the winner would then do to acknowledge the cheers of the crowd as he mounted the rostrum to collect his gold medal. I suppose he would just give a curt nod.

35

These days, being a tenor is all part of growing up

I am proposing a new soccer programme for television. It would consist only of expert analysis by Jimmy Hill and the lads and it would be left to the viewer to imagine what the match might have been like.

The Olympic Games could consist of one huge and splendid opening ceremony, full of symbolism and doves, with thousands of schoolchildren arranging themselves on the grass to spell out uplifting messages. Then everybody could go home and forget about the 100 metres, the marathon and the pole vault and suchlike inconveniences.

Lately the soccer World Cup has become an event for three tenors. It is time for everybody else to take their ball home.

It is marvellous to go into the parks these days and watch the kids kicking about a few arias together. They just put a couple of coats down on the grass and launch themselves into an energetic rendition of 'Nessun Dorma' or 'Maradona e mobile', while daydreaming that one day they will be like their great heroes Domingo, Carreras and Pavarotti.

Occasionally a fight breaks out. 'Hey, you just did a b flat,' one boy will shout. 'I never!' his friend replies. 'Yes, you did,' says the third boy. 'In that lyrical passage beginning in the fifteenth bar. I heard you.' Soon all three of them are rolling about on the ground, punching each other. In the end it sorts itself out when the fourth child, who is the conductor, threatens to take his baton home.

You have to feel sorry for the poor parents who are nagged and badgered by their young offspring to buy them the full 'kit' of white tie and tails with the super-duper screw-in shirt studs and the gold cufflinks. Then, of course, the parents are expected to haul the kids round all the major sporting events so they can listen to the tenors doing the curtain-raisers.

There are always a few spoilsports. You read from time to time of tenor-mad youngsters who have been sent home from school just because they are three or four stones overweight or because they have hit a really high note and smashed a classroom window. Some people never seem to realise that, these days, being a tenor is all part of growing up.

In this craze for tenors, the people I feel sorry for are the baritones. Unwanted and unfashionable, they do a bit of busking or just wander the country, knocking on doors asking people if they would like to hear a snatch of a song for a fiver. Usually, they are cruelly turned away. These poor wretches have become an oppressed minority. I must say, I am lending my support to the campaign for them not to be called baritones, but to be described as 'differently-octaved persons.'

It is impossible to mount an opera to employ any of these differently-octaved persons as you cannot lay your hands on the tenors for love or money – they are all booked up to sing extracts and highlights and medleys at supermarket openings, summit meetings, state occasions, the Olympic Games, company AGMs and world chess championships.

At least some of the opera houses have managed to adapt by turning themselves into elite soccer clubs. I am told by someone in the know that AFC Glyndebourne are well-placed to beat La Scala, Milan, in the European Cup this year. However, to dress up in one's finery and pay about £500 just to see and be seen at a soccer match is frankly not my idea of a good night out. If I want to see some soccer I would rather go to the Royal Festival Hall for a tenor concert and watch someone like Romario or Baggio knocking a ball about in the interval.

The marvellous tenors who entertain us these days do not, of course, confine themselves to operatic works. They also bring their genius and their vocal chords to bear on some of the great popular classics.

Those who were privileged to be present at the Ten Tenors Recital that took place just before the World Figure Skating Championships are unlikely ever to forget the brilliant performance of the marvellous Ernesto Carbonara as he sang that poignant tribute of a son to his father who, though humble in origin, though menial in trade, though simple in abode, was yet such a source of family pride. I do not believe there was a dry eye in the 100,000 audience as Carbonara milked all the emotion from those last lines of 'My Old Man's a Dustman.'

And when, as an encore, Carbonara teamed up with Luigi Pesto and Jorge Tapas to sing 'The Hands that Do Dishes Can Be Soft As your Face' followed by 'If You Like a Lot of Chocolate on Your Biscuit Join Our Club' the applause was absolutely deafening.

It was also a splendidly imaginative gesture to donate the box office takings of that recital to the Kiri Te Kanawa Fund for Distressed Sopranos.

36

Eurovision means singing from the same hymn sheet

The debate about whether Britain should take the drastic step of withdrawing from the Eurovision Song Contest has been re-opened and threatens to cause a serious split in the Conservative party. Following the weekend's Song Contest summit in Ireland, Eurovision-sceptics are pointing out the unfairness of the voting system which allows the juries of other countries to gang up on Britain, preventing the British entry from winning the Contest.

They also believe that our so-called partners in Eurovision are determined to press ahead with their scheme to have a 'single Eurovision song' by the end of this decade. Eurovision enthusiasts, on the other hand, argue that the Eurosong is the logical next step after the 'harmonisation' of songwriter-output that has been taking place over recent years. They maintain that it is important to remain at the heart of the Contest in order to help improve the tunes and the lyrics from within the Eurovision organisation.

They also argue that the sceptics are living in the past and are just suffering from nostalgia for the days of Britain's glory and of Sandie Shaw. 'The times when we could just trample barefoot on everybody else have long gone,' I was told by a member of the pro-Contest wing of the Tory party.

However, the sceptics argue that the true cost of Eurovision is now suddenly emerging. Having won the contest for the third year running, Ireland is effectively being fined £2 million. This is the estimated cost of staging the Contest in Ireland again next year as ordered by the faceless Eurovision-based bureaucrats.

What this means is that Britain's economy could be brought to its knees if the juries of, say, Portugal, Norway and

Luxembourg got together and made us the winners next year. According to the rules, we would be forced to host the Contest in this country, at enormous expense. And we would have no say about what singers and lyrics and musical arrangements would be allowed to flood into this country.

Britain would not have any power of veto over any rendition of the most depressing love songs and there would be no guarantee of sub-titles to go with those in strange languages. The BBC would have no choice but to broadcast the programme at a peak time, thus effectively undermining the unique constitutional position of the BBC Director General, Mr John Birt.

Many people have been urging the Prime Minister to take a tougher line with Eurovision, but his supporters point out that he has secured some vital concessions for Britain. Our own participants, for example, can have a slightly longer lead on their hand mike so that they can jump up and down a bit more. However the length of the lead will be reduced on a year-by-year basis to bring us in line with our partners.

In spite of vigorous denials, it is clear that the Cabinet is divided on this issue. Mr Douglas Hurd remains determinedly pro-Eurovision. A Foreign Office source set out his policy on the issue when he told me yesterday: 'Hey, hey, it's the only way; we gotta stay together till a bright new day.'

Friends of Michael Portillo, the Chief Secretary to the Treasury, gave the clearest indication yet that, when it comes to the Eurovision Song Contest, members of the Cabinet are not singing from the same hymn sheet. As one backbencher put it to me: 'We can make it on our own. I know that's true, that's why I'm telling you, so don't be blue.'

Meanwhile opposition to Eurovision is growing. The sceptics are pointing out that under terms of the Single Eurovision Act, which we have signed up to, in next year's contest, the British entrant may be forced to perform with a German or even a French backing group.

June

37

Woe-level time for parents

Q: 'The most important phase in the development of a parent occurs when his (or her) children are taking O-levels.' Discuss, giving examples where possible. Details of working and of neuroses should be shown. Marks will be awarded for owning up.

A: For about three weeks in June every year the behaviour patterns of certain parents show a marked change. Although it is their offspring who are actually taking the exams, parents put on certain 'displays' to suggest that they themselves are going through the ordeal.

One early sign of this transformation is when the parent interrupts the silence of breakfast with the question: '*Est-ce que tu as un oral exam en français cet après-midi?*' On being assured that this is indeed the case, he will then go on to seek further information and to ask questions to which he must surely already know the answer – e.g., '*As-tu un frère ou une soeur?*' or '*Où habites-tu?*' These questions should be answered patiently and calmly. It sometimes has a soothing effect if the replies are given in French.

At this time of the year many parents can be observed in the morning standing on their doorsteps shouting down the street to small figures disappearing in the far distance. 'Read the questions carefully!' they call out. 'Make sure your adjectives agree!' Sometimes, over the sound of the traffic you can hear that doom-laden cry: 'Remember your endings!'

That strange restless fluttering you hear at evening time is not the starlings preparing to roost but a million parents all saying, 'How did it go?'

Men and women in offices interrupt business and meetings to make furtive telephone calls. 'How was Geography?' they murmur. 'What do you mean, they didn't ask about igneous rocks? After all the work I put in on them?'

They settle down at night to study and to write essays on the role of Feste in *Twelfth Night*, and they leave them lying temptingly round the house where they are ignored.

It is a time of doubt. There is only one thing of which a parent is utterly convinced and that is that his child will go to school on exam day without a pen. And have they got a sharp HB pencil for multiple choice? What if the lead in the pencil breaks and causes a multiple disaster?

Meanwhile, the children who are actually sitting the O-level exams go about the business in a pale and dogged manner, untroubled by all this adult agitation. They know that their parents are being stirred by painful memories of their youth.

That valuable book, *How to Help Your Parents Through Your O-levels*, gives sound advice to young students on this subject. It suggests that they can offer a few words of reassurance to their mothers and fathers at this difficult time, to say, for example: 'Honestly, I won't feel you have let me down and I won't reproach you if I only get a D for Biology.' Or: 'Exams aren't everything, you know. You've still got your mortgage.'

Over the years, certain developments have taken place which make it more difficult for parents to interfere in O-levels. Most obviously and most distressingly, mathematics has moved on from the study of those friendly fellows Euclid and Pythagoras. Now the parent is shipwrecked in the confusion of pie charts, vectors and matrices. In the run-up to the exams there is hardly time for the child to explain these concepts to the baffled parent.

Some pupils also attempt to thwart over-eager offers of assistance by taking up weird subjects which were never in the syllabus in the good old days. They do O-levels in such things as 'Inter-Relations in World Civilisation,' or 'Telephone Answering and Diet Control' or 'The Origins of Turkish Naval Slang.'

Even then a parent can turn to other displays. The fish-paste sandwiches for packed lunches are prepared more lovingly – 'As it's Eng. Lit. (B) today, I've cut the crusts off. And any father can be counted on to stay up all night ferreting through dustbins and wastepaper baskets, clearing out wardrobes and refrigerators, un-making beds and crawling under tables to search for that vital book of German irregular verbs which has been lost. Or left behind at school.

Perhaps it would be a good idea if examiners could award grades to parents for the work they put in at O-level time. Imagine the excitement when the results come through. 'Look! I got an A for Concerned Facial Expressions! And a B for Not Mentioning Physics. Oh dear, I see my Nagging Oral let me down badly.'

Well, you have to admit it is an education. When my son was doing O-level Art and had to produce some working sketches for a painting of a building site, I did not hesitate. I put aside my notes on *Julius Caesar* and crept out of the house at 10.30 at night, borrowed a wheelbarrow from the local builder's yard and wheeled it home in the darkness. Then, wearing a cap, I posed with the wheelbarrow in front of the television set for an hour or so, then returned it to the builder's yard before its absence was noticed. All that for a C.

At least I did better posing for A-level, lounging scruffily on the grass in the park with a large cider bottle held up to my lips. That was worth a B. My most treasured academic qualification.

38

Where there's a Will, there's an A-level

What is remarkable about this new education debate started by Prince Charles is that it was actually foreshadowed by Shakespeare himself in his play, *As You Do Your Thing*. I will not burden you here with the pentameters, but some of the stage directions will be familiar.

Fanfare. Enter the Prince, followed by his courtiers, who are named after British Rail InterCity stations – Leicester, Darlington, Bristol Parkway and noble Exeter St David's. In a longish speech, the Prince bemoans 'th' illiteracy in this our Realm'. The courtiers stand in a semi-circle, solemn and stiff-shouldered, with their feet planted seven inches apart and their thumbs hooked in their belts. *Exeunt.*

Only noble Exeter St David's remains. He is tall and splendid with a fine tenor voice. Wisps of his white beard get stuck to his lips and a fine spray is caught in the beam of the footlights when he makes his speech. He rejoices that his son, Studius, is diligent and scholarly.

Good heavens! Here comes Studius now! He bounds on to the stage and embraces his father. He is accompanied by his best friend, Eruditio. They have both been away for three years at university in Italy. (They are Two Graduates of Verona).

You can tell they are best friends because they slap each other on the back a lot; this makes quite a hearty noise on the puffed-up leather jerkins that they wear. Their exits and entrances are always taken at a run because of their cheerful disposition.

A new scene. The shadowy expert educationist, Sir John Relevant, sits in his garden rebuking his pretty, breathy daughter, Academica. You can tell he is an unsympathetic character because the make-up lines on his pale face are pro-nounced and indigo. He is a widower and he dresses in black.

Academica is devoted to him, but exasperated. She wants to study for her A-levels, but Sir John says she should acquire skills. As far as he is concerned, she should be preparing for her welding days.

Secretly, Academica is taking correspondence courses. (This provides plenty of opportunity for 'business' with let-ters). And while – disguised as a boy, for some reason – she goes to the post to send off her essay on character and structure in Beaumont and Fletcher, she drops it. Studius picks it up and offers to tutor her – or him, as he believes her to be.

While wrestling with the syntax of *Gammer Gurton's Nedle* with Studius, Academica realises she is in love with him. Studius is unsure of his feelings towards the youth.

Now, the comic scene. Tom Truant and Dick Dropout do not have a single GCSE between them. To judge by their accents they are Gloucestershire cockneys.

They lounge against a piece of greengrocers' artificial grass draped over a box and construct enormously elaborate puns. The only way you can tell they are being funny is that the jokes are signalled with the words 'Marry, good Master Dropout' or 'I care not for thy curriculum, whoreson Truant.'

Sir John Relevant finds out about Academica's tutorials and forbids them. She is heartbroken, but help is at hand. A plot is hatched. The landlady of the inn frequented by intellectuals, Mistress Swiftly (heaving bosom, beauty spot, loud voice), disguises herself and wins his heart.

At their tryst, you can scarcely hear what they are saying because of the ridiculously intrusive stage whispers of Drop-out, Truant, Studius and Academica who are hiding behind a wall, eavesdropping. Mistress Swiftly tells Sir John that she could never love a man who could not conjugate the sub-junctive of the Latin verb *doceo*.

In his passion, Sir John obliges. Ahaaa! All those in hiding are delighted because Sir John has been tricked into showing himself to be a scholar, so he can no longer stop Academica pursuing her studies and her Studius.

All ends well. To the huge relief of Studius, Academica reveals herself as a girl and they will be married as soon as she gets her qualifications. Lord Exeter St David's makes a long speech giving them his blessing.

Sir John and Mistress Swiftly are betrothed and he promises to introduce her to the gerundive. Dropout and Truant agree to go to evening classes. Eruditio, who had been detained elsewhere in a sub-plot, arrives to announce that he has won a scholarship to business school. More backslapping.

A pale and intense young man plays a stringed instrument and sings a meteorological folk song. Everybody dances. Enter the Prince, who recites the sort of couplet that usually brings such proceedings to a close:

> Now this is the end of our gay revels,
> Which you will soon be studying for your A-levels.

39

Hail! Oh declining Latin lovers

The trouble with Latin as a school subject is that it has never been properly marketed. Nowadays you need to go out and *sell* this sort of thing to the choosy teenage consumers of education.

In the old days, when we were wrestling with the subjunctive and we asked a teacher or a parent what was the point of studying Latin, we were easily fobbed off with some muttered excuse. It helped us to think clearly, they said, or it was the basis of understanding European languages.

The other pretext was that it would open up such wonderful literature and poetry to us, as if every adult in the country has Virgil for bedside reading. That does not wash so well these days when anyone can watch a video of *I, Claudius*.

Now it has been announced that even the Royal Latin Grammar School in Buckingham is abandoning the teaching of Latin, after 500 years of doing so. Only six pupils put their names down for the two-year course that was due to begin in September.

O tempora, O mores, as we always remark after the second sherry at old boys' reunions.

The problem, as I say, is that not enough attention has been paid to marketing the subject. At my little advertising consultancy, Imperatives, we have been putting our heads together and kicking around a few ideas to think of a campaign that will really appeal to the kids of today.

Our slogan is: Study Latin – it's a Classic! The idea is that gerunds are fun, Pliny is a laugh a minute and conjugating is the In Thing.

We have come up with a neat logo, suitable for car stickers.

105

It says 'I love amo, amas, amat'. There is, of course, a picture of a red heart in place of the word 'love'.

The whole publicity campaign is going to be launched with a spectacular Ides of March pop concert at Wembley Stadium at which we will be selling *Et tu Brute* T-shirts. I rather like the witty poster we have designed to advertise the concert. It shows a soothsayer warning Caesar: 'Ides – don't die of ignorance'.

Of course, you need a modern hero-figure with whom the kids can identify. We are very fortunate to have secured the services of Rex Mensa, the gifted lead singer with the rock group, Ablative Absolute, who, winter quarters having been left by them, recently recorded their latest single which is set to go right to the top of the charts.

'The fans will not fully appreciate the lyrics of my song, "Oh Baby, When you Kiss me my Heart goes Wah Wah Wah" if they do not realise that I am using the vocative case to address my baby,' Relax sagely points out.

Our television commercials will consist of Vox Pop interviews. These include, for example, a young football supporter who says: 'I went to West Ham's away match in Manchester in order that I might attack the city.'

On the merchandising side we will be launching a whole new range of SPQR leisure wear with the slogan 'Go jogging like the Roman legions used to do in Gaul'. And there is our new brand of aftershave, *Veni, vidi, vici* – for the man who wants to conquer on sight.

The point we will be striving to put across is that Latin is modern, up to date and trendy. It is the 'now' subject. Latin is, as we say in the marketing business, very MCMLXXXVIII.

40

Has Oxford lost its faculties?

Nowadays I divide my time between London and Oxford, where I was recently appointed Visiting Professor of Office Politics – a post which has been more than adequately funded by a company manufacturing office coffee machines. My lectures, which are delivered in furtive whispers at the side entrance of Magdalen College, have been well attended.

The old place has changed now that the university has gone in for fund-raising in a big way, but we dons have not lost our appetite for gossip and backstabbing. The subject that is exercising us at the moment is, who will be made the first Rupert Murdoch Professor of Language and Communications? As you know, News International plc, Mr Murdoch's company, has just given £3 million to establish the chair.

I myself am attached to Didcot College (motto: 'It's the One the Discerning Undergraduates Choose') and we pride ourselves on the quality of our college intrigue. In fact, Inspector Morse comes round every week to solve the particularly grisly murders in the senior common room, and some of the Fellows are hoping he can be appointed Visiting Detective if we can get sponsorship from an ITV company.

At our self-service canteen-style high table the other evening conversation turned to the subject of a suitable candidate for the Rupert Murdoch professorship. The Master, who looks most imposing in his T-shirt with the logo of a major non-drip gloss paint company, surprised us all by suggesting that the job should go to a woman. This example of progressivism was quite out of keeping with the traditions of the college.

The woman he had in mind was Ms Sophie Toothe, an attractive undergraduate at Trinity, reading All-Time Showbiz Greats. It turned out that he was only proposing her because he was planning one of his donnish epigrams. He wanted to say: 'The Rupert Murdoch Professor of Language and Communications is very generously endowed.'

This greatly displeased the Bursar, who was campaigning on behalf of the more mature Miss Edith Anstruther, Toyota lecturer in Motorway Etiquette. This was so that the Bursar could say: 'The Rupert Murdoch Chair in Language and Communications is very well upholstered.'

I was in favour of a compromise candidate, such as the immensely distinguished Dr Ambrose Darkly, who has devoted fifteen years to translating the poems of W. H. Auden into 'rap'. Unfortunately it turned out that he had been poisoned the night before by the Senior Tutor in a dispute about the college Fax machine.

The popular TV don, Sebastian Bloke, *enfant terrible* of *Any Questions?*, pioneer in turning tutorials into multi-media experiences, and author of *Why I Say Wake Up, Dreaming Spires*, was also very much in the running, but made the mistake of putting his own name forward. Even his success in persuading thirty millionaires to make out covenants to fund the university's first video library is unlikely to overcome the hostility towards him.

Of course there is one man in our college who would be the ideal Professor of Language and Communications. Since the purpose of Mr Murdoch's gift is to encourage the study of the impact of the media on the English language, there could be no better candidate than the dauntingly scholarly J. P. S. Robertson.

He has made it his life's work to translate the classics into tabloid. He won great acclaim in academic circles for his versions of two of Shakespeare's tragedies – 'I'm No Wimp, Says Danish Royal' and 'Lovesick Romeo Mourns Love-Tug Death-Pact Gymslip Bride.' He is currently working on 'A Midsummer Night's Love-Romp.'

Personally, I think his greatest feat was to distil the whole of *Moby Dick* in one word – 'Gotcha!'

41

Farewell my lovely diploma

I know that you will be as excited as I am at the news that Loughborough University is to introduce a post-graduate course for private detectives. Successful students will get a Diploma in Investigatory Management – and then, presumably, they can put DIM after their name on the frosted glass of their office door.

I have been trying to imagine what the course will be like. There will be practical lessons in tilting trilbies, turning up raincoat collars and lighting cigarettes under street lamps, I suppose.

Many people will want to know how to get on this course, so it may be helpful to describe the progress of a typical student, a graduate in English literature, whom we will call Philip Taplow. He makes his way by train to Loughborough, then looks for the address which has been scribbled on the back of an old cigarette packet.

It is a shabby office block, and on the fifth floor he walks warily down a bare corridor until he comes to a door marked 'Admissions Tutor'. He knocks, but there is no reply. He gives the door a push and it swings open.

The room is deserted. There is an old wooden desk near the grimy window and on it is an ashtray loaded with stubs, plus an ancient telephone.

Taplow walks over to the bookshelf, picks up a volume and blows the dust off it. It is the 1978 annual report of the University Grants Committee. There is also a soiled coffee cup, but the dregs smell more like Scotch.

At that moment there are 156 brilliant white flashes followed by pitch darkness. Unseen by Taplow, the admissions tutor has tiptoed into the room and slugged him on the back of the

head with a BA gown filled with sand. Taplow is out cold. He hits the floor like a copy of *Ulysses* dropped from a great height.

Taplow has no idea how much later it is when he comes round. He has been hauled on to a chair and is looking at five members of the admissions panel who are waiting to interview him. One of them is a red-headed dame whose legs are somewhat more interesting than *Middlemarch*.

'It is customary, when regaining consciousness, to make a wisecrack, Mr Taplow,' the chairman of the committee says to him.

'My head feels like I've just spent forty-two hours in the students' union bar with Branwell Brontë,' he says. They throw a glass of water in his face and inquire about his *curriculum vitae*.

'Before this I was into English literature investigations,' he says. 'Missing persons, mostly. My last assignment was trying to track down a broad who was known as the Dark Lady of the Sonnets. There was not much to go on. The only lead I had was that there was a Mr W. H. who was involved somehow. He was the Mister Big. He had a legit business as a front operation. It was a bookshop called W. H. Smith. I hung around there for a few weeks, but nothing came up. So that's why I'm here.'

He is accepted for the course, and a month later he is back

110

in Loughborough and he is tailing a man through the mean streets. The man seems to know he is being followed and does all sorts of things to shake him off. He boards buses, then jumps off them in the middle of traffic; he goes into large buildings, then comes out of the back door disguised as a telephone engineer with a wooden leg; he jumps into the Loughborough Canal and stays under water for two hours breathing through a straw from a McDonald's milkshake.

In the end Taplow corners his man at the end of a rubbish-strewn alley. They punch each other on the jaw eighteen or nineteen times, then Taplow picks him up by the collar and throws him against the wall and watches him slide to the ground.

'Dr Maidenhead?' he says.

'Who wants to know?'

'My name is Taplow. I've come for my tutorial.'

'Not a bad effort, Taplow,' his tutor says, rubbing his jaw. 'I'll give you a B-plus for that.'

'Thank you very much.'

'Next week, I'd like you to break into my house and steal the course examination papers.'

42

Anyone for Dernk, Grernn and Aieee?

Hnneuuuch! That, I need hardly tell you, is the big first serve of the Exciting Young American at Wimbledon. It will be interesting to see if the Promising Australian can respond with a cross-court *pfwuurr*. My own expert prediction is that the first game will go something like this:

> *Hnneuuuch!*
> *Pfwuurr.*
> *Bleewallt.*
> *Dernk.*

Fifteen love.

Of course, if they were playing on a clay court the *bleewallt* would be more of a *snirraklep*, but these need not concern us here. Everybody agrees that the Exciting Young American has a very effective *bleewallt*. He has been working on it very hard in training.

I am very happy to report that my latest book, *The Phonetics of Lawn Tennis*, is being published to coincide with the opening of Wimbledon fortnight. I shall be at the All England Club in the next few days signing copies of the book, then slamming them shut with a satisfying *blap*. This is a sequel to my handbook for line judges which listed A Hundred Different Ways of Shouting 'Foot Fault.'

One of the themes of my latest book is how remarkably tennis developed over recent years. The level of fitness is so high nowadays that most of the sounds are produced by the abdominal muscles. Ten years ago, a *hooow* was a comparatively rare event, but now even the junior women players have made *herrnnnh* very much a part of their game.

112

Lavishly illustrated, the book also records some of the greatest moments of Wimbledon history. Obviously, I had to include that unforgettable nail-biting tie-break between the Unflappable Swede and the Unpredictable Czech which actually went to *fffaahhwhaughh* before it was finally decided. And there is also a chance to re-live that golden moment when the Plucky Argentinian saved match-point by retrieving a seemingly impossible *phwooon* and playing a *grernn* down the line.

The book also gives brief biographies of some of the great 'characters' of tennis, like the Rangy Brazilian, who actually had his grunt sponsored by a multi-national company of bulldozer manufacturers.

I provide a glossary of some of the technical terms used in modern tennis. Those readers who cannot afford the £54.99 for the book might care to tear out this page of the paper and refer to it when watching Wimbledon on television. This is, of course, just a sample of some of the expressions which are explained in the book.

Blollop. The Highly-Strung American has just mis-timed a simple backhand and hit the ball into the net. He has now kicked wildly at a stray ball which has dislodged the on-court microphone.

Merrrnnnn. The Unsettled English Girl is just about to try to get her second service in at love-forty and three games down when the British Airways flight to Montevideo passes overhead. The suspense is awful.

Oooooooo. The Exciting Young American has followed up his *hnneuuuch!* with a rush to the net. His opponent has also advanced and they are engaged in a quickfire duel of *werps*. Harry Carpenter is lost for words.

Nguu. The overhead smash by the Consistent Frenchman has hit the baseline judge in the solar plexus. (Nguu is also the name of the unseeded Vietnamese player who is putting up a brave show against the Unpredictable Czech and causing him some problems with his unorthodox, two-fisted backhand *splernks*.)

Aieee! Do not be deceived by this. The Teenage Italian Girl may seem to be uttering heart-rending sobs and you may feel an impulse to rush on to the court to console her, but she does not need our sympathy. She is currently demolishing the Colourful Australian Veteran with her totally ruthless serve and volley (*hnneuuuch!* and *graaak!*) game.

Woooble, whirrick, wheee! The brisk south-westerly wind is blowing directly into the umpire's microphone, the Press photographers are busy and the spectators at the match on the adjoining court are becoming over-excited. I hope all this does not affect the concentration of the Unsettled English Girl as she prepares to serve to save the match.

Ah-errr. Oh, I'm afraid it did.

Mwoonh. Pay no attention. That is just me hauling myself out of the armchair to switch the television off.

43

They also serve who only sit and fret

Well, there he is, seated on the chair resting his hands on his knees and staring at the carpet. I wonder what is going through his mind at this moment, Virginia. Perhaps he is remembering that column of a year ago when he produced two sizzling paradoxes and a pastiche in the first paragraph and then suddenly went to pieces.

Now he is approaching his typewriter. He will be wondering if he can recapture his old form. I think if he could just string a few sentences together it would give him the confidence for a fight-back. I get the feeling, Virginia, that he does not really believe in himself at the moment. He needs to get a first sentence in.

Ah, he has just successfully squirted a cherry stone into the wastepaper basket. That ought to give him a tremendous boost. Yes, he is putting a sheet of paper into the typewriter and is going through the familiar routine of tugging his earlobe. Let's see if he can produce a word now.

That next cherry stone was well wide of the wastepaper basket. As he picks that one up, and the other seventeen, he will be telling himself that he is going to have to concentrate. He is just going to have to put those cherry stones behind him and settle down to the job in hand.

He has written the word 'The'. I expect he is remembering the last time he began a column with the word 'the' and he won't want to repeat the mistakes he made on that occasion. That was when he took on the subject of alternative medicine and came to grief in the fifth paragraph and was out of the writing game for several weeks.

You can see his wife and his daughter on the sofa reserved for the writer's family. I wonder what is going through their minds at the moment, Virginia. There is nothing much they can do to lift him. In fact he did mention to them in conversation earlier that he felt he never wrote as well when they were among the spectators.

Now they are quiet for a moment as he takes three deep breaths to settle himself to write the next word. No, something on the desk has distracted him. A piece of paper. It is difficult to tell from our position but it looks like a telephone bill. He is going over to the spectators and he is appealing to them. We can't pick up what he is saying, but I only hope this is not going to be another display of temperament. Sometimes, Virginia, I think he can be his own worst enemy.

The adrenalin is really pumping now. Two more words! They are 'quick' and 'brown'. I think we can make out his strategy at this stage. On past form I would expect him to type the word 'fox' next, wouldn't you Virginia?

No, we were wrong. The next word is 'fxo'. That was a very cleverly disguised noun. He has obviously decided to exploit the element of surprise. So now we have 'The quick brown fxo'. He will be wanting to build on that.

Just as I feared, he has thrown it all away. He has screwed the paper into a ball and tossed it over his shoulder. It looks to me as if there is a bit of a cross-wind there because the ball of paper struck his daughter on the shoulder. She won't be happy about that.

He is trying to psych himself up. He has removed his shoes and is standing on one leg on the desk punching the ceiling with his fist and muttering. We can't hear what he is saying but I expect it is: 'Come on, you have really got to raise your typing and stop the rot. You fought your way back from an apparently hopeless position in October 1987 and you can do it again. You are going to have to start taking risks with longer words.

Now he has given himself a good talking to, he is at the typewriter again. Here is an interesting development. The dog has come into the room and is staring at him. I wonder what is going through the dog's mind, Virginia. It is probably thinking back to that memorable walkies of April 1988.

He has stood up again and is going over to the kettle. Goodness, the dog completely wrong-footed him there. Oh dear, there was no need for that. He surely risks a public warning for dog-abuse. I hope we are not going to see a repetition of the third re-write of the week before last.

Here is a change of tactics. He has gone into the garden and is pacing up and down on the lawn. Of course, he has never really been happy on grass, has he Virginia? I wonder what is going through his mind at this moment. I expect he is deciding to go inside and watch Wimbledon on television.

44

The man who can't give up the boos

It was truly a privilege to be granted an interview with the legendary Giovanni Ridicolo, one of the world's foremost opera booers. He has hissed in all the great opera houses and has taken the leading catcalling role in just about every major production. Nobody who witnessed him 'giving the bird' at the Metropolitan Opera House in New York last year will forget the experience.

He is in London at the moment at the start of an exciting European tour, and I went to see him last week shortly after he had taken Covent Garden by storm in *Il Trovatore*, leading the booing of the tenor Walter Donati, who was suffering from a throat infection.

Ridicolo graciously received me in his dressing room, which was decorated with lavish displays of decaying vegetables and insulting telegrams from well-wishers and from some of the greatest names in the jeering fraternity. 'Look what the cat dragged in,' he said to me, instantly putting me at my ease.

What, I asked, was the most taxing role he had ever played? 'That is an extremely banal question, if I may say so,' he replied.

'Thank you very much.'

'I suppose it must be in Sturzacker's *Die Unglückliche Kartoffel*,' he went on. 'The opera lasts for five and a half hours and it requires great discipline to avoid being lulled into a state of amiability in Sturzacker's more lyric passages so that you cannot rise to the climax of derision at the curtain call.'

I ventured to ask him his opinion of Wolfgang Erstenacht, who is said to be able to scoff in several languages and who is reckoned to be Ridicolo's greatest rival. 'Pfui,' he said with a dismissive wave of the hand. 'The man is nothing but a heckler.' He suggested that Erstenacht would be more at home in the House of Commons than in the auditoria of the great opera houses of Europe. 'Of course, we are the best of friends,' he added.

Ridicolo's career has been an extraordinary one. He was first spotted coughing and fidgeting in the audience at an amateur production of *Iolanthe*. Within two years he was being fêted in Salzburg, where they named a tuna fish salad after him, and he was soon the darling of the brickbat buffs in Paris. By the age of twenty-six he had fulfilled his great ambition to boo at La Scala.

He has always said that the finest performer he has ever booed opposite was the fabulous soprano booer, Lotte Schriek. 'She could also whistle piercingly between her thumb and forefinger,' he recalled. 'She did this once in Act II of *Prosciutto di Parma* at the Vienna Staatsoper and within three minutes eighteen taxis and five small dogs had arrived on the stage, disrupting Stracciatella's aria in the poignant peppermill scene.'

A highlight of Ridicolo's career was the curtain call at the end of *Nodino di Vitello* in 1986. He warmly applauded the singers and the conductor. Everybody was astonished when he politely clapped the director. The suspense became unbearable when he even rewarded the designer with lukewarm applause. Suddenly he burst into a frenzy of booing at the box office manager! Everybody agreed that it was a *tour de force*.

He has always been keen to push back the frontiers of his art. Some purists were shocked by his venture into the 'pop' world last year when he delivered his memorable rendition of 'What a Load of Rubbish' at an Arsenal v. Tottenham Hotspur football match. 'It was a very good experience to involve the young people,' he said. For relaxation he still sometimes indulges in a little slow hand-clapping when Yorkshire are playing cricket.

Earlier this year there were amazing scenes in Munich. Suddenly five rows of the stalls turned and actually started booing Ridicolo. In a moment the principal singers had joined in and were hissing venomously, then the conductor turned and started making eloquently insulting gestures at him. 'It was a very moving tribute,' Ridicolo said.

Our conversation was interrupted by a knock on the dressing room door and a voice calling 'Three minutes to curtain call, Signor Ridicolo.'

The great man got to his feet and took off his elegant silk dressing gown. 'Oh well,' he said, with typically disarming modesty. 'I must go and blow my little raspberry.'

'Break a leg,' I replied warmly.

July

45

Putting the horror into horoscopes

So, did you manage to scrape through last Thursday? This was the day when a disobliging configuration of Mars and Saturn was supposed to cause general all-round ghastliness. Aquarians, in particular, were supposed to have a Black Thursday and Leos would wish they had never been born – or, at least, not born between July 24 and August 23.

I survived somehow, thanks to a sustained spell of dedicated cowering, interspersed with periods of flinching. At least it made a change from the usual horoscope unease. The problem is in living up to the astrologers' expectations. 'For too long you have allowed close associates to take you for granted,' they sniff. 'It is the time to face the facts about a financial matter,' they say, though you get the feeling that they suspect you are not up to it. 'This could be a decisive period.'

These horoscopes always seem to assume that one leads a complicated life with more seething undercurrents and show-downs than a soap opera. :'You cannot remain silent any longer,' they say. 'A confrontation with a loved one may be painful, but you will emerge stronger and wiser,' they tell you. 'Although you have an axe to grind, you must be careful not to cut off your nose to spite your face.'

Does anybody really live like this? Yes, of course they do. This is exactly how astrologers live. I went to call on my good friend Sylvester Wagstaffe (a.k.a. Madame Zabaglione) and I asked him kindly to describe a typical day.

'At about eight o'clock in the morning my nearest and dear-est wakes me with a cup of tea,' he said. 'This can be a dis-appointment on the home front. A loved one has put sugar in my tea, as she has done for the past fourteen years, in spite of the fact that I do not take sugar. I decide that it is time to bring matters out into the open. I do so, and difficulties of an emotional nature ensue.

'After breakfast I take Rover, my close associate, for a walk in pastures new. Unfortunately, on the way back, Rover catches sight of the cat which is the loved one of our neighbour, Mrs Talbot. The dog and the cat find themselves at odds. This is something of a reversal for the cat and relations with Mrs Talbot are likely to be clouded for some time to come. No amount of pouring oil on troubled waters will alleviate this situation.

'I leave home and make my way to the office. There are many challenging aspects to this journey and I have to be prepared to take a few knocks. When I arrive at the office, my superior reads the riot act. This augurs a professional setback. I suspect he is somewhat out of sorts because of his emotional ties with his secretary, Amaryllis. She, it seems, is seeking fresh horizons. With regard to my superior's affairs of the heart, this is likely to prove a major stumbling block. I believe he has been hoping for a long-term involvement.

'My superior orders me to realise my full potential, so I go to my desk to accomplish the tasks before me and prepare the horoscopes. My colleague, Mr Pringle, comes over and says some things can no longer be left unsaid. I suggest that he resists the temptation to settle old scores. And he retorts that there is little to be said for continuing to make allowances for the failings of others. Money matters are to the fore, a debt has to be repaid and assets change hands.

'What people fail to realise about me is that my ruling planet, Jupiter, has no joint financial arrangement with me. This challenging aspect is going to compel me to sort out my priorities in no uncertain terms.

'In the afternoon working relationships show no sign of improvement. My superior suggests that if I am not careful I may experience a major alteration in the working pattern of my life. This is another area of discord that has come to light. The encouraging aspect is that it is nearly five o'clock and time to make the homeward journey.

'However, when I reach the domestic setting I find that my euphoria is short-lived. The clear implication of a note waiting for me on the mantelpiece is that my nearest and dearest has ceased to be my partner. After a reappraisal of her lifestyle she has decided to run off with her close companion, a part-time water diviner. This news radically alters my outlook. My normally ebullient nature is somewhat unsettled. With only a dog as an associate, I find my emotions coming too close to the surface. I retire to bed, wondering what tomorrow may bring.'

46

Just desserts

It is reported that some restaurants are facing bankruptcy because so many people are booking tables and then failing to show up. I think I can throw some light on this matter. It is almost certain that the people responsible are a loosely-bound but militant group known as the Lunch Saboteurs. I have been monitoring their activities for some years.

For muddled ideological reasons, the Lunch Saboteurs dedicate their lives to messing up simple arrangements to meet for a meal. They may well be a slightly more moderate break-away faction of the Hungry Brigade, which was responsible for many restaurant atrocities in the 1960s – including a wave of indiscriminate soup-spilling.

There are certain tell-tale signs that give away the Lunch Saboteur. 'We must have lunch,' he announces in an emphatic tone that does not suggest an invitation so much as an iron law. The entries in his diary are busy and feverish.

A training manual of the group has fallen into my hands. After selecting his victim and arranging the meeting, the Lunch Saboteur is instructed to introduce complications. First of all, the time and place for the lunch are changed four or five times. Then, when the victim is suitably confused, the Preposterous Suggestion is made.

'Look, I've just discovered that I have got to be in Barnstaple on Thursday. Why don't we meet up there and then go on to Exeter together?' Or: 'You don't mind if I bring along my vet and his wife, do you? Only he has been so good about speeding up my hamster's hip-replacement operation.'

It was J. P. S. Hodgkinson, the shadowy guru and theoretician of the movement, who coined the ingenious paradox: 'A true Lunch Saboteur is more creative than a master chef.' His other famous saying is: 'The empty chair at the table for two has all the subtle flavour of a *quenelle de brochet*.'

Over the years I have drawn up a top-secret dossier on the activities of the Saboteurs which I am prepared to hand over to the Restaurateurs' Association of Great Britain in exchange for, say, an *artichaut vinaigrette*.

The Location Ploy is frequently used. You spend an hour waiting fretfully at the Thoughtful Quiche and then *he* insists that you had definitely agreed to meet at the Café des Ennemis. Should you happen to meet up, he will get a telephone call in the restaurant from someone who is waiting for him at the Trattoria Sciatica.

On May 11, 1982, Raymond Stansfield, a noted tactician in the Lunch Saboteurs movement, had people expecting him in sixteen restaurants in London and a wine bar in Broadstairs.

I was the victim of two other successful operations by Raymond Stansfield. He offered to take me by car to a restaurant in Chelsea, so I confidently made the booking. Then, suddenly, he insisted on making a diversion to distant North London to collect a wicker chair he was having repaired. Three traffic jams later we just had time to get a sandwich at a pub in Finchley, leaving a head waiter cursing me in Chelsea.

On another occasion, as we were sitting down to eat, he made a great performance of spotting eight friends (co-conspirators) cleverly scattered around the restaurant. After an upheaval of furniture moving – 'Can we just push these tables together?' – there were places for nine. 'You sit over there, Oliver, and we'll wave to you from time to time.'

Those of us who persistently fall prey to the Lunch Saboteur and sit alone, toying self-consciously with the first course, belong to an altogether more high-minded group known as Friends of the Hors d'Oeuvre. We linger over the prawn cocktail and become increasingly pessimistic about the chances of our guest making the *entrée*.

Attending party conferences in recent years, I noticed that the issue that aroused most fervour among the journalists was where to go out to eat in the evening, and, even more important, whom to go with. Naturally, many of them wanted to have Sir Robin Day in their group. Because he was so benign and anxious never to give offence, and perhaps also because he was non-committal in the sweetest way, a large number of people were convinced that he had accepted their invitation.

At scores of restaurant tables all over Brighton or Blackpool you would see one empty place, and the great cry went up to head waiters all over town: 'We're expecting Sir Robin.' Head waiters in Blackpool and Brighton are justly famed for their scepticism. I have always thought that, 'We're Expecting Sir Robin' would make a good title for a rather poignant poem.

It is said that restaurateurs are now planning dreadful revenge on those inconsiderate people who book tables and do not show up. They claim, for example, that booking a table represents a contract in law. It would be wise, therefore, to get your solicitor to make the booking for you. 'My client would like a table for three in a quiet corner and without prejudice.'

Restaurateurs are also taking credit-card numbers with the bookings and then charging the accounts of the no-showers for meals they might have had. This could raise some interesting philosophical questions.

Will they add on a 15 per cent service charge for the waiter who hovered so attentively at the empty table? Might a tiresome and litigious customer try to sue a restaurateur for defamation of character? 'You have stated that, had I turned up for the meal, I would have chosen the halibut. This is a disgraceful slur. And you are implying to my credit-card company that I am the sort of person who would order a cheap, inferior Liebfraumilch, thus damaging my credit rating.'

Restaurants that are persistently jilted are entitled to seek some redress, but I fear that these measures may lead to an escalation in the activities of the Lunch Saboteurs. Smouldering discontent could turn into something *flambée*.

47

Quick dip into the art of dunking

The hundredth birthday of the digestive biscuit was marked yesterday with a fascinating article in the *Daily Telegraph* about that particular delicacy and its inventor, the Scottish baker Alexander Grant.

I was already aware of this anniversary as it has considerable relevance to a study I have been pursuing into the art of dunking. My illustrated coffee table book on the development of dunking over the centuries, entitled *Immersed In History*, is published next month.

Many people are under the mistaken impression that dunking is merely the furtively genteel act of softening a biscuit by dipping it in a cup of tea or coffee. There is a feeling that it is 'not quite nice'. This was the attitude taken by the Victorians and, alas, it still survives. My research shows it was not always so.

Dunking was invented in France at the beginning of the eighteenth century by none other than the Comtesse d'Unque. She was widowed at the age of twenty-three and a great beauty.

Apparently, she was being courted by a wealthy merchant who was much older than herself, and one day when he came to call she noticed that he was having difficulty eating the rather hard and over-baked biscuits on offer because he had no teeth.

Delicately, the Comtesse took a biscuit, dipped it in her cup of chocolate and nibbled it. The grateful suitor followed her example. He was so overcome by her tact and her beauty that he married her, settled all his wealth on her and died two days after the wedding.

Dunking became the rage in the smart salons of Paris.

Aristocratic ladies would employ 'dunking masters' to teach them how to do it elegantly. Important questions of etiquette arose, such as, to what depth should a biscuit be dipped into the coffee? The rule emerged that it should go no deeper than the length of the top joint of a lady's little finger.

Circular biscuits had to be dunked and nibbled round the rim, working in an anti-clockwise direction. Oblong biscuits were to be approached from the bottom left-hand corner.

Incidentally, the Comtesse d'Unque was related by marriage to the Bourbons, but the two families had been bitter enemies for generations over a disputed inheritance. There was a saying in France, *'Les d'Unques and les Bourbons ne vont pas ensemble'*, meaning literally 'the d'Unques and the Bourbons don't go together'. This was later distorted into the old rule, 'Never dunk a bourbon'.

Dunking found its way to England and became fashionable among young bloods. It was also the cause of a famous duel in 1774 between the dashing young Earl of Hainault and Lord Robert Bakerloo.

The Earl was with a group of cronies in a coffee house in the Strand when he leant over to a nearby table where Lord Robert was sitting and impudently dunked his biscuit in Lord Robert's cup. At the ensuing duel, the Earl's life was saved when the Bath Oliver biscuit he kept in his breast pocket stopped the ball from Lord Robert's pistol.

Towards the end of the eighteenth century ladies were using elegant silver 'dunking tongs' to hold the biscuit as they dipped it in their cup. These Georgian dunking tongs nowadays fetch very good prices at auction.

As the custom spread to other classes in the Victorian age it ceased to be considered smart. There was the great dunking

strike in Oldham in 1862 when factory workers, who were issued with one rock-hard ginger nut every other Thursday, tried to make the biscuits more edible by dunking them.

They were promptly sacked and the strike that was called in their support lasted fourteen weeks.

The arrival of the digestive biscuit threw the whole thing into confusion. Traditionalists felt it was too soft for dunking. It was also inclined to dissolve and leave a tell-tale gooey brown sediment at the bottom of the cup. A Victorian father who found evidence that his daughter had been engaging in the shameful practice of dunking would throw her out of the house. As the poor girl crept away he would shout after her: 'And take the biscuit!'

48

All burnt up breathing in the barbie fall-out

The barbecue season got into its stride at the weekend. This is good news for me because my new book, *Passive Barbecuing*, is to be published soon. In this book, I go into the various aspects of inhaling other people's barbecue smoke as it wafts about the neighbourhood. I tackle the issue of 'aroma cholesterol' and whether you can dangerously increase your intake of animal fats by sniffing somebody else's barbecued pork sausages a mile away upwind.

In an absolutely fascinating chapter, I also consider the all-important environmental side effects. I have been able to establish scientifically that in the summer months a 'marinade cloud' forms in the atmosphere above this country. All the ingredients that go into marinading the meat evaporate in the heat of the barbecue, are then carried upwards and finally come together again in clouds above the earth.

Tests have shown that these are now affecting our weather pattern. Parts of Wiltshire have been found to be suffering from 'marinade rain' caused by clouds formed by barbecues in Hampshire and drifting across on the wind, causing some ill feeling between the two counties.

In the Salisbury area, the rain is found to have an artificial hickory-smoked flavour. This is getting into the grass on which the cattle graze and giving the milk and cheese an unusual taste. There has been a different sort of marinade rain in Cheshire. Tiny droplets of tomato ketchup, lemon juice and various spices have been falling in this area.

Some of this has come down on clothes on washing lines, and there have been cases of people so overcome by the appetising smell of their washing that they have tried to eat it. A Blackpool youth who went to the doctor complaining of stomach ache was found to have consumed three flavoured pillowcases.

Some environmentalists have suggested that if we have a long dry summer these droplets could turn to dust and we could have what look like red sandstorms but which are clouds of cayenne pepper.

As well as the tasty smoke, the other thing that drifts across from nearby barbecues is the conversation – or snatches of dialogue like 'I could have another chop, if pressed' or 'sangria – how clever!'

The voices carry, and it is all a bit theatrical. In fact barbecues, being rather public events, tend to turn into performances. In the evening they can have special lighting.

All this explains why I have written my first full-length barbecue stage play. It is a searing drama about lust, and power and minor burns. The wonderful thing about this idea is that the audience is lured into the theatre by the smell of the glowing briquettes. Later on, they are held there, transfixed in their seats, by the enticing aroma of barbecuing which lingers in the stalls.

In the first act we witness the power struggle of the two principal male characters as they jockey for position to see who will put on the foolish apron and supervise the cooking. From a theatrical point of view, the great thing about a barbecue is that people have to eat in relays as there is never enough food ready at the same time. This means that a couple of the characters on the stage may be reduced to eye-rolling speechlessness by the scorching chop in their mouth, but the others can always keep the dialogue going. There is also some eloquent mime.

Characters rush off stage from time to time, and you can never tell whether it is out of an excess of pent-up emotion or a need to spit their hot dog cinder into the lily pond.

One of the dramatic devices I have used is to have the heroine stuck in one of those awkward canvas chairs that she cannot lever herself out of because of the plate on her lap and the glass in her hand. Meanwhile, her lover is being unfaithful with her best friend, Fiona, and wandering off into the darkness on the pretext of looking for Fiona's lost flip-flop sandal.

There is an amazing climax with a duel with kebab skewers

and the revelation that the unfaithful lover has unwittingly eaten the flip-flop, which was char-grilled by Fiona's cuckolded and vengeful husband. Watch out for this powerful play when it opens in the West End. It is called *Don't Let the Burgers Get You Down*.

49

Wash and Go

There is clearly a strong link between hairdressing and travel. When you go for a wash and blow dry, whatever the time of year, they always say 'Had your holidays yet?' Or: 'Been anywhere nice?' In answer to your own muffled question from the depths of the towel, you learn that they have indeed been somewhere nice. Bali actually. With a friend. Or California. With the fiancé. Yes, actually it was their fourth visit. On the whole, though, they prefer the Seychelles.

There is something about cutting hair that gives people a wanderlust. It could be the effect of spending the whole day circling people in a chair and snipping.

All this has made me wonder if some of the great travellers of history were, in fact, hairdressers. Did Marco Polo perhaps journey to the Far East and visit Kubla Khan, the Mongol emperor, to set up a salon? Perhaps he called it something jokey like 'A Load of Old Kublas.' Circumstantial evidence now suggests that Christopher Columbus's first act, on discovering America, was to open an upmarket establishment called Isabella's.

Recently my theories were confirmed when, quite by chance, I found a battered old book in a junk shop. Although the pages were mouldy and yellowing and the ink had faded I could decipher enough to see that it was the journal of an expedition in Africa in 1871 led by Sir Mortimer Unisex, the noted society hairdresser of Victorian times.

On the journey he had two lieutenants, Michael and Leonard, and he was also accompanied by three formidable young ladies named Lisa, Joanne and Cheryl. They made the arduous trek on foot, but their baggage was carried by a faithful mule called Vidal.

If I may, I'll read you some extracts from this fascinating journal. This one begins: 'April the second in the year of Our Lord eighteen hundred and seventy-one. Somewhere in Africa. As we had finished our magazines, I determined that our party should move off. I told the others it was time to wash and go. We set out in good heart. Then, as we were passing the basin of a river whose name I do not know, we were attacked by a band of savages. Happily, Lisa, Joanne and Cheryl were able to overpower them by seizing them by the shoulders and pushing their heads down into the basin. They said "Water all right for you?" but the savages could make no reply as they were eaten by small voracious fishes.'

Here is another entry for a few days later: 'The sun glinting on our scissors attracted a group of natives. They indicated that the headman of their village wished to parley with me. I said I could fit him in at 4.30 in the afternoon as I had a cancellation by the headman of another village. At the appointed hour we found him seated on his primitive throne with a sheet-like garment draped round his shoulders. Michael held a mirror in front of him and Leonard held one behind him and said 'How's that?' The headman was amazed at the magic that enabled him to see the back of his own head. He presented me with his most beautiful daughter and I said she could be my receptionist.'

The expedition got tougher. A week or so later we find this terse entry: 'Supplies of conditioner running low. Cheryl is in a bad way. I have said nothing, for fear of lowering the morale of the party, but I suspect it may be dry scalp.'

Then there is this extraordinary entry. 'Today, after travelling for many months, often in appalling conditions, we came across a white man in the bush. He was somewhat dishevelled and distracted and it was difficult to discern where his parting was supposed to be. He came towards me with his hand outstretched and said: "Dr Livingstone, I presume."

'I informed him that he presumed wrong and that I was Sir Mortimer Unisex. He said his name was Stanley and, although he had shown up without an appointment, Lisa agreed to give him a trim. He departed well satisfied and said he would ask for Lisa next time.'

The last entry in the journal says, 'Extraordinary coincidence! Met another white man today. He said his name was David Livingstone. 'Oh yes,' I replied. 'Been anywhere nice?'

Rowena's novel is set to climb steeply into the bestseller lists and I am told that several major airlines are interested in bidding for the in-flight movie rights.

50

Holiday where you like, strikers are holding a nap hand

As usual at this time of year, I am providing my European Strike Update Service for readers going on holiday abroad. This prepares people for industrial disputes that may be taking place in the area they have chosen.

The Federation of Balearic Chambermaids are due to begin their campaign of non-cooperation this Thursday. This will affect people staying at hotels in Majorca. Chambermaids will be ignoring all 'Do Not Disturb' notices and barging into bedrooms at all hours of day. It is a complicated and long-running dispute partly concerned with 'soap money.' Traditionally, the chambermaids have been entitled to thirteen seventeenths of the proceeds of all partly-used bars of soap from the bathrooms which are sold for re-cycling. Managements want to reduce the share to nine fifteenths.

They also want to abolish the chambermaids' traditional 'sand bonus' whereby they are paid extra for every gramme of sand they collect from shoes left in guests' bedrooms. If the dispute escalates, the chambermaids, led by the fiery Dolores Napas, are threatening to block hotel corridors with their trolleys, brooms and heaps of dirty linen so that holiday-makers will not be able to leave their rooms.

People visiting Greece should remember that July 28th is Goatherds' Day of Action on all Greek islands except Bathos where goatherd supervisors will be used to keep flocks together. In other places the day of action will have a knock-on effect as it will take some time for all the goats to be rounded up again.

A mass meeting of Costa Brava swimming-pool supervisory staff decided last night that next week they would be coming out in sympathy with the sunshade adjusters who have been on strike over the recruitment of low-paid semi-skilled adjusters who, they say, are putting holiday-makers' lives at risk. 'We are just waiting for a shade to come sliding down its pole and hit somebody on the head,' said strike leader Jaime Napez.

This latest vote means that there will be nobody to skim dead insects and leaves off the surface of pools.

After 100 days, the Italian ice-cube strike is no nearer settlement, and the Federation of Tuscany Peppermill Operatives are continuing to work to rule and refusing to do more than three twists at any one time. 'It's up to management to make a move,' said the Federation's leader Giovanni Napio. 'We want to see more money on the red and white check tablecloth.'

As you probably know already, all members of the French Union of Terrace Bar Waiters downed trays as from noon yesterday. This is part of a long demarcation dispute with the behind-the-bar staff over who should have the job of putting the little tear in the till receipt when the customer pays for drinks. 'I have never seen the lads so surly,' said waiters' leader Jean Nappe.

Motorists planning to drive in France should remember that after August 4th the gendarmes on point duty at crossroads are beginning their indefinite 'campaign of dramatic but unintelligible gestures.' They claim they were promised a 15 per cent pay rise for increasing their productivity by blowing their whistles twenty-eight times a minute. If the French Interior Ministry carries out its threat to replace the point duty officers with supervisors from the National Academy of Mime it is likely that the traffic light maintenance engineers will be called out on strike.

Efforts to mediate in the unofficial cargo handlers strike in Tenerife are continuing, but in the meantime the men are refusing to touch fifteen crates of sun-block cream which are stuck at the airport. Portuguese unions, by the way, have switched National Don't Speak English Day to August 14th. The Provence postal workers boycott of postcards is still in force and unlikely to end before October.

And, of course, it is as well to remember that all Italian churches and monuments are still being picketed by the two-hour photographic processing workers. They are claiming that they should be paid extra for putting those little 'quality control' stickers on prints.

If you are reading this in an airport departure lounge, I am sure you will agree that it is just as well to be forewarned of these troublespots so that you can fully enjoy your holiday.

51

Unimagined heights of literary passion

Airport literature has always been a despised art form; indeed, it is a handy term of abuse if you want to wound an author. Those paperbacks we grab at Gatwick or Heathrow, to be read on some distant beach, tend to be a predictable choice. A bestseller list compiled by the British Airports Authority is headed by a thriller by John Grisham, followed by Jack Higgins, Gerald Seymour and Danielle Steel. Martyn Goff, soon to be chairman of the Book Trust, called this list disappointing. 'It seems that people are buying books as they would cornflakes,' he said.

All this is changing. Now that the airports have managed to improve the quality of their sticky buns and coffee, they are taking steps to raise the literary tone as well. The idea is for airports to produce their own literature, instead of the airport shops buying it in from the publishers.

I understand that they have already appointed a writer-in-residence in the departure lounge of Terminal 3 at Heathrow. In fact they have appointed two – one smoking and one non-smoking.

Miss Natasha Puffe, the smoking author, has just completed the final draft of her 790-page epic, which is entitled *Listen for Further Announcements*. It traces the history of five generations of a Yorkshire family living in the corner of a departure lounge and waiting to be called for a delayed flight to Tenerife.

Miss Puffe served her apprenticeship carrying out security checks and searching passengers' hand luggage. 'You learn a lot about human nature when you rummage through people's overnight cases,' she told me. 'You discover what makes them tick. It has been an invaluable experience for me as a writer.'

Non-smoker Gavin Fitt has nearly completed *Long Haul*, which is an account of one man, Arthur Grimwade, who makes the long, long journey on foot from the departure lounge to Gate 17 to board his flight. It describes the hardships he encounters on the way, the people he meets and the obsession that drives him on to his goal.

He never makes it. He collapses from exhaustion just next to Gate 12, and as he loses consciousness he hears the words on the public address system: 'Last call for Arthur Grimwade, passenger on Flight 702 for Frankfurt, please come to Gate 17 immediately . . .'

Gavin Fitt told me: 'The book is very much a voyage of discovery. At the end you feel that although Arthur never reaches his destination, he has, in a very real sense, found himself.'

There is now a terrific buzz about Heathrow's literary revival: the airport has become as exciting as Bloomsbury was in its day. Soon it is likely to become a place of pilgrimage, with people from all over the world arriving to see where great literary figures queued to check in or stood and gazed yearningly at the departure board, in search of inspiration.

Another acclaimed Heathrow author is Rowena Carton, who used to work in the Duty-Free Shop, but decided to get out of the rat-race and, as she put it, 'reject the crude materialism of it all'. Now she is to be found every day at the Tastee Bite snack outlet at the airport, which has become the haunt of all the leading writers, artists and Bohemians.

Rowena Carton's first novel is likely to become a classic of airport romantic literature. It is called *He Claimed My Heart*, and it tells the story of Rupert and Miranda, who have just returned from a holiday in the Algarve. While they are waiting in the baggage reclaim area for their cases to be unloaded from the plane and placed on the carousel, Miranda finds herself standing next to Pierre, who has come in on the delayed flight from Paris.

A spark flashes between them. With barely a word, they decide there and then to elope. Rupert is left staring forlornly at the carousel on which Miranda's abandoned tartan holdall is going round and round for ever, nestling against the elegant pigskin suitcase that belongs to Pierre.

142

'Heathrow provides such a conducive atmosphere for the creative process,' Rowena told me. 'You can feel your imagination take flight.'

52

Farewell the Bible, palm trees and Brahms

I always used to wonder in the old days of *Desert Island Discs* what would actually happen to those cosy celebrities when they landed on their BBC atoll. It was fascinating to speculate about their fate after they had been waved goodbye by the courtly Roy Plomley and were left alone with their eight records, their worthy tome and their luxury – 'something of no practical value' as Mr Plomley always so politely insisted.

Now that Michael Parkinson, his successor, is to quit as presenter of this long-running radio programme, the BBC is reported to be looking for somebody else to take over the show. This is a mistake. What we need is a new concept.

That is why I have devised a programme called *Desert Island Discomforts*.

The idea is that I would rescue these celebrities from their desert island, bring them back to the studio and interview them about their experiences.

'Did you find that music played a big part in your life on the island?'

'Well, of course, music has always meant a great deal to me, but after a fortnight those eight records were driving me crazy.'

'Was it difficult for you to pick the record which annoyed you most?'

'Goodness, yes. It was a frightfully difficult choice. The Vivaldi seemed to attract the sand-flies and make them bite more viciously, but I suppose, if you pressed me, I would have to say that the disc I most regretted was the Brahms.'

'I remember you telling Roy Plomley that you were quite good with your hands; quite a practical sort of person. Why did your rude shelter collapse?'

144

'I built a sort of hut, using the gramophone and the Bible and the Shakespeare which were already on the island. Then, for the roof, I used my luxury, the easel and canvasses. The whole structure fell down when I lost my temper and hurled the Brahms against the wall.'

'I seem to recall you saying that you would take Gibbon's *Decline and Fall of the Roman Empire* as your favourite book because it had always meant so much to you. How far did you get through it before you realised it meant nothing to you at all?'

'I got half way down page 31. Then I wished I had been honest and asked for *Winnie The Pooh*.'

'And how did you get on with Shakespeare and the Bible?'

'After the hut fell down I threw them both at the seagulls because they kept reminding me of the signature tune of the programme.'

'You said at the time that you would not try to escape because you were a contemplative and self-sufficient sort of person. How long did it take before you cracked?'

'On the third day I hailed a passing boat which was carrying a BBC television crew making a drama documentary. They said they could not take me on board because of cut-backs in their budget. Fortunately, I was able to send a message in a bottle to my agent who managed to get me released from the desert island clause in my contract.'

'In all your time on the island what was it that you missed most about civilisation?'

'Oh, the little things. Like fame. And being interviewed respectfully on the radio.'

53

The isle is full of big noises

The first thing I did after being wash'd up on the shore of this horrible desolate island was to get down on my knees and give thanks to my Maker for my deliv'rance from the great storm. Though much amaz'd and discompos'd in my mind, it seems I have suffer'd no great injury in my adventures, save for the fact that I am much troubl'd by apostrophes.

Day Four. I esteem my present condition very miserable. This morning I ate nothing but a few wild plants that tast'd much like radicchio and this only serv'd to fill me with bitter regrets that I was not dining in the congenial company of my friends Giles and Deborah in Hampstead. I play'd my record of Beethoven's 'Ode to Joy', but it gave me little respite from my gloom, the sound quality being but a poor thing compar'd to mine own quadrophonic system back in the sitting room of my house in my belov'd and sorely miss'd Kensington.

The sun in the day being very hot, I resolv'd to build myself a shelter. The only materials to hand were my easel and the canvasses. Tho' repenting sorely of my falsehood in saying that I desir'd nothing more than to pass my solitary days in oil painting, I was pleas'd that I had been granted these materials. I squeez'd out the tubes of oil paint to seal the cracks in the roof. Apostrophes still troubling me.

Day Nine. I awoke in the middle of last night and observ'd a figure in the darkness going through the heap of my poor belongings outside my shelter. I seiz'd one of my oil painting brushes and leap'd upon the brute, thrusting the sharp end into his throat. The wretch submitted. Babbling, he explain'd that he was looking for 'a good read'. He hoped to find a book by Jeffrey Archer or Catherine Cookson. 'The only books you can get on this island are J. R. R. Tolkien's *Lord of the Rings*,

146

or *War and Peace*, or Proust,' he said. He took out my copy of *Tristram Shandy* and threw it impatiently on to the ground.

He said he was Sir Swanley Orpington, the hugely admired and famous Shakespearean actor. 'I shall call you Friday,' I said. 'No, call me Thursday; I'll be out Friday,' he replied, explaining that this was a joke that was always very successful on chat shows. Today I left my record of Ella Fitzgerald singing 'Manhattan' out in the sun so that I was able to bend it into a serviceable sun-hat which I glued to my head with some leftover oil paint. Apostrophes somewhat improv'd.

Day Thirty-Six. Today I went down to the shore where I saw a most melancholy sight. There on the sand were the skulls and bones of celebrities who had tried to escape back to civilisation and to *Wogan*. They had fashioned their record-players into flimsy craft and these had founder'd on the coral reef. There were also charred remains of manuscripts which had been used for camp fires by those people who had brought writing materials as their luxury.

'We worship Sue Lawley,' Friday told me. I agreed that she was frightfully nice. 'No, she is a goddess,' he said. He took me to a clearing where there was an immense statue of a woman with elegant legs. I was astonish'd to see a crowd of people in rags with long hair shuffling round the statue chanting 'Yes, music has always been important to me' and 'This one's a bit of nostalgia, really'. I thought I recognised Lord

Callaghan, Edward Fox, Jane Asher and Antonia Byatt, Susannah York and Melvyn Bragg in the throng.

There is another group on the most westerly point of the island who worship Roy Plomley. Friday tells me that sometimes there are wars between the Plomleyites and the Lawleyites and they hurl copies of *The Complete Works of Shakespeare* at each other. In the hills there are said to be small, desperate bands of Parkinsonites.

As I write this journal by the light of my smouldering record of Bob Dylan singing 'Blowin' in the Wind' I can hear the distant strains of 'My Way' from the other side of the island, mingled with the eerie howls of half-crazed celebrities.

Day Fifty-eight. Last night my camp was attacked by a gang of Sinatra-worshippers, a most hellish group of brutish degenerates. I kept them at bay by playing my Vivaldi record. My discomposure has return'd and I greatly fear another outbreak of apostrophes.

Day One Hundred and Sixty-two. This day I have resolv'd to return to Britain so that I may appear on *Any Questions*. I went about the whole island collecting copies of *The Decline and Fall of the Roman Empire* which I have lashed together to make a raft. My record of Rod Stewart singing 'Sailing' will serve as a paddle. Tomorrow I begin my perilous journey.

148

54

You're going to have to let me go

For me, one of the highlights of the Summer Season, better than Henley and smarter than the Royal Academy private view is the period of Speculation about a Cabinet Re-Shuffle. This is when the chattering classes put on their summer outfits and start telling each other that so-and-so is not happy at the Ministry of Hazards and Health Warnings, another is likely to be moved sideways and a third is due for promotion after sterling work at the Department of Safe Pairs of Hands.

The most enjoyable part of it all is the exchange of letters when a Minister obligingly resigns. These have become such works of art that I am reliably informed that many ambitious men and women try to get on in politics just so that they can write one of these resignation letters. They then have it framed and hung on the wall of their new office in the merchant bank.

Dear Miss Angela Trumpet, When you asked me to meet you at the Happy Caterpillar Salad Bar today, you explained to me that you needed 'new blood' in your love life if you were to continue to make progress towards becoming a fully rounded person in the difficult years leading up to your twenty-fifth birthday.

You indicated that you felt that it was necessary to make a change in lifestyle policy, with less emphasis on walks in the countryside and visits to folk festivals and a greater concentration on drinking margaritas in nightclubs and driving at 85 m.p.h. in open-topped cars. In these circumstances, I quite understand that there is no longer room for me in your affections and I am therefore tendering my resignation. I should like to add that it has been a privilege to serve as your boyfriend. Yours sincerely, James Starfish.

Dear Jim, Thank you for your typically generous letter. I shall always remember the marvellous work you did in the cause of finding 'the real me' and I am grateful for the unstinting support you gave when I got locked out of my flat. Silvio joins me in sending best wishes to you and to Hermione, your goldfish. Love, Angie.

Dear Landlord of the Rising Sun, I was pleased that we were able to have our 'clear the air' talk last night. I absolutely respect your conviction that I gave you a £5 note for a bitter shandy and a packet of dry-roasted nuts, just as I am sure you respect my firm belief that it was a £10 note. I understand that this is an issue of principle and that you feel that it would be best if I were barred for life from the Rising Sun. I am grateful for the opportunities you have given me to quench my thirst in your pub and to listen to many interesting anecdotes there – and for the enjoyable ploughman's lunches. Yours sincerely, James Starfish.

Dear Mr Starfish, Thank you for your letter. It is with great regret that I learned that I had barred you for life from the Rising Sun. I wish you good fortune when you take your custom elsewhere. I should like to take the opportunity to put on record my gratitude to you for helping the Rising Sun through to the quarter finals of the Inter-Pub Quiz in 1991, and particularly for the way you remembered the name of the Prime Minister of Belgium. Cheers, Bob Browning.

Dear Bank Manageress, When you called me in today to discuss my overdraft I was interested to hear that you were 'not running a charity here'. As you know, my employers recently felt obliged to tender me my P45 as I was regretfully severing my links with the company and leaving my job by mutual agreement to seek fresh challenges and pastures new. This is why funds are not forthcoming. I fully appreciate your need to bounce my cheques at this time and would like to thank you for your patience up to now. Yours, James Starfish.

Dear Mr Saftrish, Thank you for your most kind letter. Our regular meetings about your overdraft have been among the most rewarding experiences of my time as manageress of this branch. My staff join me in sending good wishes to Hermione, the goldfish. You are being charged £35 for this letter. Yrs, Julie Sissons (Ms).

Dear Electricity Board Manager, Yesterday you informed me that you were cutting off my supply of electricity, due to non-payment of overdue account. You were kind enough to explain to me that the electricity board's policy of holding down the peak-rate tariff could not be sustained if customers did not pay promptly. I am a full supporter of this policy, so naturally I accept the need to terminate my supplies. May I say how much I have enjoyed using my electrical appliances – particularly the food processor. Yours ever, James Starfish.

Dear Customer No. 453/90ZZ803, We are very pleased to hear that we have your continued support in supplying cheap, clean, reliable energy to domestic premises, excluding your own. Thank you for the units you have used. Our computer wishes to be remembered to your goldfish. Best wishes, ELEBOARD.

Dear Prime Minister, Thank you for offering me the post of junior minister in the Department of Health Hazards. I look forward to a fruitful and lasting association. Yours sincerely, Jim Starfish.

August

55

It was just a Lucky escape

It has been a while since I last saw Lord Lucan. Well, that is
not strictly true; I did actually see him last Tuesday, but not
to speak to. He was coming out of Victoria Station. I spotted
him just in time, nipped down the stairs into the Underground
and mingled in the crowd. You get quite good at this sort of
thing. It's like a sixth sense; you know that he is somewhere
around.

Our first meeting took place about a year ago. I was seated
at a pavement table of a wine bar in west London when this
man took the spare seat. He had a Harrods carrier bag with
him and I could tell he wanted to get into conversation; he
did all the tricks, sighing with pleasure after every sip of
Chardonnay, chuckling occasionally, shifting his chair,
leaning over to read my newspaper.

'Bet you can't guess who I am,' he said at last.

'Give in,' I replied, holding the newspaper a little higher.

'Here's a clue: I'm Lucky.'

It took five minutes to establish that he really was the Missing Earl. 'Ask me about that fateful night in November 1974
when I disappeared after the murder of the nanny,' he said
eagerly. 'Let me tell you my extraordinary story of those missing years and how the trail went cold and how I gave the
police the slip. Now at last it can be told.'

The carrier bag was full of all his old press cuttings. He
tipped them on to the table; they were crumpled and greasy.
He had changed very little from the photographs in those
cuttings. The Earl began his tale: 'The events of that night,
nineteen years ago, are so vivid in my memory that it might
have been only yesterday . . .'

I said I was just going to get myself another glass of wine.

Inside the wine bar, I slipped through a door marked Private; it led to a storeroom. I squeezed through a window and jumped down into a narrow alley, climbed over a wall. As I ran across a patch of waste ground I heard his voice calling after me: 'Hey, come back. I've got to the bit where I hide up in the woods and build myself a rude shelter out of branches . . .'

The next day the telephone rang at 6 a.m. I recognised the voice. 'My heart was in my mouth. Would some alert policeman see through my nun's disguise?' I slammed down the phone, threw some clothes into a bag and left the house.

Since then I have been on the run from Lord Lucan, changing my appearance, using different names, keeping on the move. It has not been easy. My tight circle of disloyal friends have put up a 'wall of chatter' giving the Earl far too many clues to my whereabouts.

Once, when working as a waiter in a rough roadside diner in Guatemala and going under the name of Raimondo, I looked up and saw that dapper figure with the distinctive moustache and the Harrods carrier bag walking purposefully towards me. 'So, in this frail craft, I hoisted sail and set out to sea, not knowing when I might next see land.' Dropping the plate of chilli con carne I was carrying, I leapt through the window of the diner and clambered aboard a passing lorry.

In the months that followed I usually managed to keep one step ahead of the Earl. Once, at an isolated airfield in Ghana where I was about to board a plane for the capital, I walked into the Customs shed and caught sight of the back view of the familiar figure. 'The simple inhabitants of the island seemed to treat me as some kind of god,' he was saying. The Customs officers were half asleep and did not notice me as I tiptoed out of the shed. Even though I had never flown a plane before, I managed to get a light aircraft to take off; and when I crashed in the mountains half an hour or so later, I was not too badly hurt. I staggered to a village where I was well received and my wounds were dressed.

Back in Britain, I live out of a suitcase, moving between different lodgings, posing as a salesman of aromatherapy products. Sometimes, at night, I look out of the window and see this figure with a Harrods bag lurking in the shadows in the street below.

Last night the telephone rang. 'Hi, there!' a man said. 'Voice from the past – it's Ronnie Biggs.' It is clear that I am going to have to lie doggo for a while longer.

56

Don't ask me to desert my post

It is a splendid thing that Terry Waite has drawn attention to the importance of the postcard. Lately it has become a rather despised form of communication, good only for banal and dutiful messages from holiday. There is no doubt that on numerous occasions, postcards have changed people's lives.

I remember when I was going through a low period how I was helped by a postcard that arrived out of the blue. It was from the local library. It said: 'The following books were due for return on June 13, 1988, and you are asked to return them as soon as possible.' Underneath, the librarian (whom I scarcely knew) had added this message in her own handwriting: 'J. L. Drew and R. G. Wagstaffe: A History of Northumbrian Agricultural Implements.'

This certainly helped to pull me through. I wasted three days searching the house for the book, then I sat down and tried to make a list of all the things I knew about Northumbrian agricultural implements. This list was so short that I concluded that I had never read the book. It took six months to discover that my best friend, Neville, had stolen my library ticket and was borrowing obscure volumes in order to lay a false trail. The good thing about this experience was that it led, indirectly, to my well-known abiding interest in Northumbrian agricultural implements.

No doubt many readers have had similar experiences. You dodge into a small art gallery to avoid an old school friend and five years later you are still getting postcards from the gallery inviting you to a private view of Serge Sanderstead's exhibition of 'Collages and Interesting Bits of Dead Thistle, Autumn 1991.'

The nice thing about postcards is that they don't challenge

you intellectually. They often have the word 'Postcard' printed on them so that there is no confusion about what they are. And there is usually a vertical line to make it clear which side you should put the message and which side you should write the address. This can be very helpful: when you receive a postcard it is quite easy to read your own address and find it much more interesting than the message.

The other brilliant thing postcard publishers do is to print a small rectangle to show you where to put the stamp. Marvellous. And how ungrateful of the postal authorities of the nations of the world not to issue stamps that actually fit these rectangles. What a shame when your postcard home from Greenland needs two stamps, but has only one rectangle.

Sometimes, to be really helpful, they print an instruction inside the rectangle. 'Affix stamp here,' it says. 'Affix' is one of my very favourite verbs; it is used almost exclusively by printers of postcards and of particularly tiresome forms. I think we should liberate this verb, show it around a bit, let it see life. Let us say: 'Hey I've got my big toe affixed in the hot tap,' or 'Affix 'em up! This gun is loaded.'

Of course, everybody agrees that it is permissible to read the messages on other people's postcards. They are, as we say, in the public domain. People are not inclined to conduct their adulteries by postcard and they are not a thrilling read. If we don't mind reading the postcards of others it's odd that we don't *add* to them. I know of only one instance. Our friend Cynthia Throwley sent us a postcard from Paris. It was a picture of Notre Dame and the eloquent message was: 'This place is absolutely terrific!!!' A few words had been added. 'If you don't mind me saying so, I think Rheims is a much finer example of Gothic architecture. Yours faithfully, L. Catchpole, Sorting Office.'

There ought to be scope for embellishing holiday postcards at source. In the Cannes hotel, you could sneak up to the postcard that someone has slaved over all day and append (there's another good verb) a couple of lines. 'Betty and Bob *say* weather fine and all well, but they have been fighting like cats on the terrace every evening.'

Incidentally, this is not widely known but a postcard is believed to have had an important influence on the life of John

Bunyan. His cousin was on a touring holiday around England and sent him a postcard which inspired him to write *Pilgrim's Progress*. The rather smudgy picture on it was, according to the caption on the other side, 'Slough of Despond at Low Tide'. His cousin had written in the space reserved for messages these simple words. 'Enjoying a good break. Looked round City of Destruction yesterday and planning to move on to Valley of Humiliation tomorrow a.m. Hope all well with you.' Well, that's my story and I'm affixing to it.

57

Posted overseas

A postcard has arrived from our dear friends, Hugo and Sophie Fender, who are on holiday in Mauvais-les-Bains. Well, to be strictly accurate, it is from Sophie, but Hugo (who, I am thrilled to learn, has 'gone quite brown') sends his regards.

I rush upstairs to share the exciting news with my wife. 'Hotel comfortable,' I announce breathlessly, bursting into the room. 'Journey not too bad, considering.' She has scarcely had time to recover from her astonishment at all this when I give her the other amazing details. 'Weather v. hot, but a bit cloudy on Thurs a.m.,' I can reveal.

'Interesting church which we have not visited yet,' my wife reads out after snatching the card from me. 'Must close now as Pernod beckons.'

The picture on the other side of the card shows the 'historic' market square of Mauvais-les-Bains. Sophie has not been able to spread herself in writing to us because the card has to accommodate five postage stamps and a printed message saying 'The historic market square of Mauvais-les-Bains' in five languages.

We spend a few moments admiring the confident way Sophie has written 'Grande Bretagne' at the end of our address and remembering their holiday last year on a Greek island when she wrote 'Anglia' in Greek letters and impressed us so much.

I can remember their Greek holiday vividly. Hugo went quite brown, the hotel was comfortable, the journey not too bad, considering, and ouzo beckoned. There were also quite a lot of Greek stamps.

Far be it from me to appear ungrateful to Sophie and Hugo,

but I do find the holiday postcard a rather unsatisfactory method of communication. Actually, knowing Hugo, I am a little surprised he doesn't send me a Telex or Fax the hotel menu to me instead.

Those pictures on the cards manage to convey very little. A harbour at night with a lot of twinkling lights reflected on the water; an impossibly green mountain against a preposterously blue sky; a dazzlingly white tower block with a kidney-shaped swimming pool in the foreground. A bit of national costume, perhaps. Or a girl in a very small bikini ('We have met some very pleasant people').

Then there is the black and white photograph of a primitive figurine in the local museum with the mystifying message on the other side: 'Remind you of anyone??!!!!'

The disturbing thing about receiving these messages from abroad is that you know that writing postcards is either a painful duty, or a holiday penance, or a pretext for sitting down in a café and not joining everyone else in the improving expedition to the fascinating old monastery.

And there is the pain of composition. You cannot tell everyone back in England that the hotel is comfortable and the journey not too bad, considering, because they may all gather to compare postcards and charge you with blatant lack of originality. So the hotel is also 'a home from home', the journey 'surprisingly trouble-free' and Hugo is 'turning a peculiar shade of pink'.

The answer to the great postcard dilemma came to me in a flash the other day. It is quite simple: postcards are going in the *wrong direction*. We who are stuck at home should be sending cards to the people who are away on holiday. It is obvious. Anybody who is away is bursting to know what is going on at home. They need to be kept in touch and they long to be reassured. The missive from Sophie is not just a holiday-maker's duty; it is a cry for help.

Yesterday, I bought a picture postcard of a Beefeater at the Tower of London and sat down to write to Hugo and Sophie Fender in Mauvais-les-Bains. 'House quite comfortable,' I said. 'Journey to work still very troublesome. Weather v. changeable, so not getting brown. Have had some excellent meals and have been keeping up with exciting developments in *EastEnders*. Will tell all when you return. Must close now, as number 38 bus beckons.'

And I am planning to organise a colour postcard of the Crankshaw's house with an impossibly green front lawn and a preposterously blue sky and a little arrow pointing to an upstairs window marked 'Your room'. I shall send it to them in Spain.

'House plants you asked me to water going quite brown,' I shall say. 'Vet says your cat comfortable. Am saving up your daily delivery of newspapers so you can catch up with all the news when you get back. Envelopes delivered to your house by postman all quite brown. Squatters not too bad, considering. Must close now as your burglar alarm beckons.'

Our friends the Wellbeloveds are away on one of their enterprising foreign trips, avoiding all the tourist traps, roughing it and visiting archeological sites in remoter parts of Turkey. I know that they would like to hear what things are like back here.

I am sending them a postcard showing a photograph of commuters (in native costume) at Esher railway station. 'We saw people just like this yesterday!' I am writing. 'They are quite reserved, but friendly enough when you win their trust. Language no problem, though we sometimes find ourselves gesticulating quite a lot. No tummy troubles so far, touch wood, and we are getting quite a taste for the beer. Dug up a fascinating old potato in the garden. Bet you wish you were here.'

And to Giles, who is on his usual lotus-eating, beachcombing, back-to-nature fortnight on a tiny dot of Pacific island, I am sending a postcard saying: 'Financial Times Share Index stands at 1,839.9 – down 22.7. Interest rates up. Economy overheating. Return at once.'

58

The fine writing is on the wall

Many thousands of people have written imploring me to produce my own list of recommended summer holiday reading. So here goes:

The Notice on the Back of the Hotel Bedroom Door. This is an old favourite of mine. The terms and conditions of stay always make a good, solid read. I like the way they are presented with the important-looking stamp of the local tourist authority. Of course, *Notice* is also a demanding work; you have got to take trouble to get the full meaning from it. Since the lighting in most Continental hotels consists of a 17-watt bulb, it is difficult to make out the words. Standing behind the door with your face pressed close to it can be a problem when your spouse bursts into the room, having just made use of the *en suite* facilities.

There is a disturbing, enigmatic quality about this work. In the chapter entitled 'Tariff' they often fill in the price of the room in handwriting. On the Continent, it is impossible to distinguish between the figure 4 and the figure 7. Thus, the delicious sense of unease is sustained right up to the moment when you are settling your bill.

You may also find in your hotel room *Instructions for Operating Air Conditioning System.* Personally, I would not recommend this one to anybody except those who have read Professor Stephen Hawking's *A Brief History of Time* and found it a doddle. This may be prejudice on my part. I've never really been able to get to grips with *Important Notice to Users of Electric Razors*, which has had something of a cult following.

The In-Flight Magazine is a must. Take it with you when you get off the plane. When you are lying in the darkened room in the evening, suffering from siesta-guilt, with the after-taste of too-real salami in your mouth, there is nothing better than to turn to this slim volume and to be carried away in your imagination to distant lands, by such items as 'Winnipeg: a Bargain Hunter's Paradise' or 'Colourful Rugs Made in Norway'.

The Lift also gives great pleasure. Most hotel lifts now have plenty of reading matter on the walls. There's a coloured photograph of a beaming chef brandishing a knife in Our Gourmet Restaurant and Buffet, which is on the ground floor next to the Conference Facilities. As your room is on the second, the journey is too short to read beyond the *hors d'oeuvres* in the sample menu.

At the same time, you are distracted by the sub-plot. There is a photograph of two women in the hotel's Sauna. A masseuse is kneading the shoulders of a woman whose head is turned towards the camera. Both are wearing tea-party smiles. They are up to something; they are plotting to murder the chef and to dispose of his body under that mountain of what appears to be Russian salad in the photograph of the Gourmet Restaurant and Buffet.

Dosage never fails to reward the attentive reader. These are the instructions on the packet of diarrhoea tablets which are printed in impossibly small type. You can't decipher the words by the light of the 17-watt bulb in the hotel bedroom, but if you take the box outside, the brightness of the sun reduces the size of your pupils to pin-points and reading is out of the question. The answer is to take it to the bathroom and read it backwards in that mirror that magnifies your pores, memorise the words and then murmur them to yourself as you watch the sun setting over the harbour.

I will certainly be reading *Other People's Headlines* on holiday abroad this year. It is the usual problem of news-starvation. Seated at the terrace bar I'll be peering at the copy of *Le Figaro*, 20 feet away, being read by the portly man with the hairy back. From this I will get only the vaguest inklings of developments in Tunisie, Les Etats-Unis, Croatie, and those jumbled acronyms ONU and Sida. This is what makes *Other People's Headlines* so elusive, yet so compelling.

A popular read again this year is sure to be *Notes Left in a*

Borrowed Villa. These are those helpful instructions left around for visitors, such as 'To get hot water, turn knob sharply to left and kick cistern' or 'Good shove and yank needed to operate loo' or 'When electricity fails, hammer on door of Antonio down the street. He can work his miracles.' All this builds up a terrific atmosphere of suppressed violence and of being on the edge of disaster.

There is one piece of writing I vow every year to leave behind, but at some relaxed moment I'll reach into my pocket and find it there – *No Milk for Next Two Weeks.*

59

Soundbites on the seashore

Last week we were treated to newspaper photographs of the Health Secretary, Virginia Bottomley, and her clan taking their annual seaside holiday on the Isle of Wight. Ninety-four members of the family gathered this year. What is it like to be among them? A clue may be found in a document that has fallen into my hands. It is called *The Secret Holiday Diary of Adrian Bottomley 14½*.

Monday. I have been hauled down here again for Cousin Virginia's annual family photo-opportunity. Tried to get out of it, but no joy. As there are 94 of us, there is always a horrendous queue for the bathroom. Cousin Virginia says the average waiting time for use of the bathroom is now two hours, seven minutes and 43 seconds, which is an improvement on last year, and she hopes to bring it down to one-and-a-half hours by the end of the decade. There are special provisions for 'priority cases' to jump the queue.

As there is not enough room for all of us in the house, I am sleeping in a tent in the garden with two press officers from the Department of Health. We are next to the BBC Outside Broadcast Unit, which is here in case Cousin Virginia wishes to address the nation. Am not expecting to get much sleep, what with the endless droning noise of BBC staff complaining about the John Birt reign of terror.

Tuesday. Ghastly night. Kept awake hours by the din of 93 members of the family munching raw carrots. Cousin Virginia was up at 6 a.m. hammering on the BBC van asking them if they wanted a comment from her on any topic.

In the morning we had a rehearsal for the spontaneous, relaxed family photograph to be taken by the newspapers on Wednesday. I got into trouble because the slogan on my

T-shirt was not upbeat enough. One of the press officers lent me a spare, with the message: 'Apples are Tremendous Fun.'

Wednesday. *Quel fiasco!!!* Another deeply dreadful night. Flashing lights outside the tent. I went to investigate and discovered it was the brilliant white teeth of 93 members of the Bottomley tribe gleaming in the moonlight.

After the photo-opportunity I had an accident. In my bare feet I trod on an empty can of export lager left behind by one of the photographers. There was a lot of blood. Cousin Virginia went into action at once. She had 40 members of the family writing out notices saying: 'Beware of Stepping on Sharp Objects' and all the others had to draw up educational leaflets entitled: 'Be Safe: When Walking About Be Sure to Wear Shoes.' Meanwhile, I was losing blood at the rate of 36 litres a minute.

Cousin Virginia explained that the family spent more money in real terms on plaster than any other family in the entire history of the universe, but we didn't actually have any at the moment. Fortunately, a passing family of holidaymakers came to my rescue. Virginia told me this was 'care in the community' and was a Good Thing.

I was very touched when *Newsnight* telephoned to ask how my foot was. Cousin Virginia took the call.

Thursday. Another v. bad night. Was woken at 2 a.m. by three officials from the Department of the Environment's Building Inspectorate blundering into the tent. They had been sent here on stand-by in case the media require pictures of Cousin Virginia making a sandcastle.

In the afternoon we were ordered to assemble at the dockside to see off Muriel, a distant Bottomley, who had been banished from the island after being seen smoking a cigarette. It's a bit hard on Muriel. After all, she is 47½. Actually, watching her sailing away, I envied her.

Friday. Hideous night. Department of Health press officers bickering with Department of Environment officials over territorial rights on groundsheet. Cousin Virginia took us all for a walk along the beach 'looking for soundbites'. She saw a man treading water 100 yards out to sea and thought it was John Humphrys of the *Today* programme, so swam out to offer him an interview. The man was so surprised that he swallowed

15 gallons of sea and Virginia managed to chivvy him ashore, telling him not to be a burden on lifesaving services.

Saturday. Worst night ever. Press officers slaving over news release, 'Health Secretary Saves Drowning Man'. I have a spot on the side of my nose but I don't intend to mention it to anyone.

60

Enter, prints charming

At this time of year there is nothing more pleasant than to stroll down to the local chemists and hang round the photographic counter where they promise to have holiday snaps developed and printed in less than a trice.

Instant processing is the thing. Returning holidaymakers stand by the counter, still jingling pesetas in the pockets of their skimpy shorts and still giving off a whiff of Ambre Solaire.

Last year, in response to an obvious demand, I set up an Instant Holiday Photo Admiring Service. I stood in the chemists and undertook to go through anyone's 24 exposures in less than two minutes, while saying, 'Isn't the sea blue?' and 'That's very good of Daphne'.

I became fascinated by this one-hour developing and printing business. You can actually watch the production line with the people doing their jobs against the clock. One day I went and took photographs of them all at work.

I got to know them. There was Craig, the team leader, who dealt with the customer and filled in the slips. There was Cheryl who sliced up the strips of negatives and hung them on the line to dry. There was Malcolm who wore white gloves and sorted out the prints as they came out of the machine. It was his mournful task to attach those quality-control stickers which said it was not the processor's fault that the pictures of the interiors of churches and bistros had not come out properly.

'Even though you see people's snaps for just a few moments you get very involved,' Malcolm told me. 'You care about the success of their holiday; it hurts when their photo of a fishing boat comes out all lopsided. You go home emotionally drained, wondering what accident occurred when the camera was dropped, letting in light and marring the quality of the pictures.'

Even in instant processing, relationships can develop. Not long ago, Cheryl fell in love with a negative. I mean she saw a picture of a young man only in negative and knew at once that he was the one for her. He appeared in some photographs of a cycling holiday in East Anglia.

Cheryl made an excuse to stand by Malcolm and she watched the prints travelling upside-down through the machine. Even upside-down, there was something special about the young man. She caught a glimpse of the slip he handed in to Craig when he collected the prints. His name was R. Tomlinson.

Every day she prayed that R. Tomlinson would return and order enlargements. Her prayers were answered. She managed to get to the counter to serve him. 'Matt or glossy?' she breathed, fearing that even the people in toiletries would hear the pounding of her heart.

'Matt,' he said flatly. But she still dared to hope he cared. Then he came in another day and handed a film to Craig. Cheryl heard him say: 'Get these done as quickly as possible, please. They are pictures of my engagement party.'

Cheryl saw the photos. They showed R. Tomlinson in a restaurant with a lot of jolly people. He had his arm round a girl. He didn't seem to care that she had luminous red eyeballs. When he came back, he smiled at Cheryl, but her eyes were filled with tears and he was just a blur.

After that they had to transfer her to the medicines counter. She still works there, but she is unlikely to serve you; she still pines for R. Tomlinson and it is impossible to catch her attention.

61

The fears of tears among my souvenirs

Here we are, halfway through our foreign holiday in unspoilt Myopia, and already I am beginning to brood. It is ridiculous. Nothing could be more delightful than this place. From our hotel just outside the quaint capital, Anadin, we have marvellous views of the sea and the fishing boats and of the olive groves on the hillside, and the Myopian people seem to be genuinely pleased to see us.

Somehow, I just can't stop worrying about the Boughton-Malherbes. Jeremy and Candida Boughton-Malherbe always bring us back such witty presents from their holidays abroad.

Last night, after the most impressive *son et lumière* in the ruins of the Cathedral of St Apoplexia, I was lying awake trying to remember all the things we have given them over the years.

There have been, I reckon, three bottles of pale yellow liqueur with a bit of twig inside, one odd-shaped bottle containing a colourless spirit with a picture of three plums (or sloes) on the label, one bag of sweets that looked like pebbles and one bag of pebbles that looked like sweets. We have also plied them with mule blankets.

The great problem is that the present must not look like a souvenir. I found a marvellous piece of authentic pottery yesterday that I thought would be just the thing for Jeremy and Candida. It was a sort of bowl that was not entirely round and it had a pattern of blurred tadpoles on it. It was not until I got it back to the hotel that I discovered that it had 'a present from Myopia' printed on the bottom. I tried to scrape it off with one of the hotel coat-hangers but the dish broke.

My wife is dreadful on holiday. She behaves like a tourist; she marches into the souvenir shops and browses and rootles without shame; she spends minutes on end looking at the displays of postcards. I lurk in the background fearing that her conduct will blow my cover, that people will not be convinced that I am a native of Myopia, that I have come into town from one of the outlying villages where I earn a modest wage selecting suitable twigs to put in bottles of pale yellow liqueur.

Postcards are a problem, too. In fact, on this holiday, I am still suffering from a writer's block over what to say to the Boughton-Malherbes. Above all, it must not be banal or facetious. I think I have found the right card: I got it in the National Museum of Myopia and it shows part of a skeleton dug up in the southern suburbs of Anadin, of a Myopian warrior killed in the 1252 Dyspepsian invasion of the country. It is either that or a black and white photograph of the crypt of St Eric in the cathedral of St Apoplexia.

The message is going to have to be pithy. On both postcards the picture is identified in five languages, leaving little room for anything else. I thought of just writing 'Feeling renewed' but I decided this might appear pretentious. The other problem is that I am going to have to be a bit terse with the Boughton-Malherbes' address because the Myopian 35-adrenalin stamp is ridiculously large. It depicts, incidentally, a native flowering shrub which I suspect also provides the twigs for sticking into the bottles of pale yellow liqueur.

We had a delicious dinner at the Café Paracetemol down by the harbour the other night. I tried the local delicacy – lizard marinaded with juniper berries and covered with sprigs of the flowering shrub. I thought we might take a tin of it for Jeremy and Candida, but these things never taste quite so good back in England. The same goes, alas, for the record of Myopian folk songs which sounded so wonderful under the stars on Tuesday, but you really need a few glasses of the pale yellow liqueur inside you to put you in the mood.

I am determined not to let the problem ruin my holiday this time. I am going to try not to worry. Perhaps it would be best to buy them a bottle of something duty-free on the plane and take them a twig to stick in it.

173

62

He's down and out, hit for six figures by the match referee

The most impressive aspect of the last Test match between England and South Africa was the consistently high level of fines imposed on the players. Apart from £1,250 from Michael Atherton and the £165 from the South African bowler Fanie de Villiers for dissent, all the members on both teams had some of their wages stopped for slow play.

This made it a most memorable match. The system of fining is giving cricket an exciting new dimension; there is a real buzz around the ground when the crowd watches a top player forking out large sums of money. I hope *Wisden*, the cricketing almanac will publish league tables of fines paid instead of all those boring old batting and bowling averages.

Actually, it could mean that players revert to being amateurs as they find, after mildly demurring at a couple of decisions and perhaps wistfully shaking their heads, that their day's wages have been whittled down to zero.

Looking back in tranquillity over this past season, I can recall some truly magical moments in the marvellous English game of spotting infringements and making people pay for them. Yes, it is that evocative summer sound of tongue on teeth as people tut-tut at cricket matches.

I shall treasure the memory of the most brilliant innings by that consummate batsman, the left handed G. W. R. Billington. He scored 23 runs and notched up a total of £2,765 in fines, mostly for raising his left eyebrow at the umpire. Then, in a wonderfully debonair way, he signalled to the pavilion for somebody to bring him a new cheque book.

He then turned to the man fielding at silly mid off, pulled a face likely to bring the game into disrepute and, on the spot, wrote out a cheque for a £1,000. All the spectators stood up to applaud the stylish flourish with which he put down his signature. Incidentally, when I said Billington was left-handed, I meant, of course, that he wrote his cheques left-handed; he batted in the normal right-handed way.

I was lucky enough to be present at the match when that terrifying fast bowler, L. M. S. Blenkinsop actually paid in £3,000 worth of fines in advance. This was a neat bit of games-manship as it was a warning to everyone that he was going to be surly, full of dissent, difficult, and probably would not even say thank you nicely when the umpire gave him back his sweater at the end of the over. The ploy worked; Blenkinsop took five wickets and came away with £150 in change.

The veteran batsman, L. N. E. R. Braithwaite is almost certainly the first player to be out 'declared bankrupt.' It happened in the match against Mid-Glamorgan when Braithwaite was scoring slowly but knocking up the fines at a brisk rate.

In the lunch interval he had to rush home and sell his house to raise the money that he owed the authorities for several hostile glances, for two outbreaks of sceptical laughter, for blatant eye-rolling and uncalled for head shaking and for per-sistently negative body language.

Even though his wife started going out to work in the third over after lunch to keep the family solvent and Braithwaite sold his pads and his boots to raise money while he was still at the crease, it was all to no avail. The slip fielders appealed that Braithwaite was 'looking askance' and, after a replay of his facial expression on the TV monitors, the umpires agreed and he was fined £750. As he could not pay this on the spot he was obliged to make his way back to the pavilion.

It was a harsh but fair decision to fine him an additional £500 for walking back too slowly and also for having 'shoulders drooping in an insubordinate manner.'

The new fines have helped players to keep on their toes. The useful all-rounder S. R. Bradshaw found himself in hot water when he happened to meet the umpire Tubby Torque-mada on the way to a match at the delightful West Norfolk ground. 'Nice day,' said Tubby and Bradshaw foolishly replied 'I beg to differ.' He quickly found himself £600 out of pocket and facing a three-match suspension.

Tubby himself was heavily fined in another controversial

incident this season. He was deemed to have held up his index finger in an inappropriately gleeful manner when giving a man out LBW. When told of the fine he made the serious mistake of shaking his head in disbelief.

63

So long to rain over us

The most marvellously evocative smell of the British summer is that warm, musty odour of damp marquee. And, of course, the most evocative sound is that crackle of rain on canvas.

After some years of marquee-sniffing, I reckon I have become quite a connoisseur. I was at a rather squelchy school sports day recently when I was stopped in my tracks as I walked past the tea tent. 'The Abercrombie wedding, June 1987,' I said to myself. The smell was unmistakable – the whiff of a particular minute fungoid organism (found only in Wiltshire) that thrives on sodden tents, combined with the aroma of freesias and coronation chicken. The contractor who supplied the marquee later confirmed my findings.

On another occasion, in Yorkshire, I identified a marquee that had been used as a hospitality tent at Henley the previous year. I just caught the giveaway smell of Pimms, damp Samsonite briefcase and a hint of Vick.

Yes, those years of 'treading the duckboards' have been good to me. My book of great rained-off events of history, *To All in Tents*, has been a steady success. And it was while tripping over a supporting rope of a marquee carrying a plate of fussily arranged cucumber sandwiches that I thought up my money-spinning musical, *Guys and Doilies*.

It was the famous downpour at the Conservative garden party in Utter Wittering the month before last that led to the discovery of this country's most promising athlete, Louisa Guttering. She was in the car park and her fiancé Gerald said: 'OK Louisa, let's make a dash for it.'

The head coach of the Harrogate Harriers happened to be passing and now Louisa is down for the 80 metres dash in the

Barcelona Olympics. When she competes she wears high-heeled turquoise shoes; with one hand she holds her wide-brimmed Guernsey cream-coloured hat on to her head and in the other she clutches her turquoise gloves. As she runs she screams 'Wheeeee!' and Gerald waits for her on the other side of the finishing tape with a nice big G and T. Everybody has high hopes that Louisa will win the gold in the Olympics provided it is a good wet day when the final of the 80 metres is run.

Another person who 'made it' through the rain was undoubtedly my old friend Keith Renoir, a distant relation of the celebrated artist Auguste Renoir. Following the example of his Impressionist kinsman who painted *Les Parapluies*, Keith produced that wonderfully colourful picture, *Les Golfing Umbrellas*.

It is not widely known that the little black clouds that are stuck on TV weather maps were designed by Katie Freshwater, the graphic artist. I started a correspondence with her a few years ago when I wrote to ask her why the little diagonal dotted lines, denoting rain, always went top right to bottom left and never in the other direction.

Katie holds the copyright on these little black clouds. She gets 0.0014p every time one of them appears over East Anglia and 0.0017p every time one appears over Devon. It may not look like much, but it mounts up. You will get some idea when I tell you that she was able to buy Keith Renoir's *Les Golfing Umbrellas* for £886,000 at Sotheby's recently.

It was because rain has been so good to all of us that I decided to hold a special pluvial celebration last week. I was delighted that the Rev. Clement Inclement could be there. It was he, you remember, who invented the sound system that squawks back at minor celebrities who open fêtes. His autobiography recently appeared in two hilarious volumes – *Village Hall if Wet* and *Just Blow Into the Mike*.

We also had those remarkable 88-year-old twins Elsie and Ivy Truscott who are the great-great-great nieces of Josiah Truscott, believed to be the first person in England ever to have uttered the words, 'Well, I suppose the farmers will be pleased.'

Musical entertainment was provided by Shem, Ham and

Japheth, of the rock group 'Sons of Noah' whose recent single, 'All I Need is Three Hundred Cubits of Gopher Wood', very nearly made it into the charts.

The pluvial celebration was judged a great success. Unfortunately, the rain held off for the day, but we did not allow that to spoil our pleasure.

September

64

A Yank with a bird at Oxford

Yes, I did know Bill Clinton when he was a Rhodes Scholar at Oxford. We were at different colleges but became close friends. I vividly recall our first meeting. Bill was in his rooms at University College, tenderly caring for a sparrow with a broken wing at the time. I had just been to a meeting of a dining club, the Absolutely Ghastly Society, and Honkers Chuffington and I had decided to go round to Univ and mob up the Yank.

As we burst into his rooms we were stopped in our tracks by the sight of Bill Clinton holding the wounded bird in the palm of his hand and gently stroking it. Honkers was absolutely overcome. He muttered something about a 'gentle giant' and burst into tears. The sparrow had been struck by a copy of Bertrand Russell's *Principia Mathematica*, which had been thrown out of a window of the Bodleian Library. Bill had made a tiny splint from a sliver of his 'oak' and was deftly tying it on with a thread from the tassel of his mortar board.

Afterwards the sparrow became devoted to Bill. It followed him everywhere and even sat on his shoulder in lectures. He called it Abe, after his hero Abraham Lincoln. All animals and birds seemed to like Bill.

All through that glorious summer the Boy from Arkansas and I got to know each other better. Our punting expeditions on the Cherwell were rather chaotic affairs because Bill was always diving overboard to save children from drowning. As I led him dripping back to his rooms he would say: 'Promise you won't tell anybody about this, Oliver.'

A group of us used to meet in Bill's rooms, sit on the floor drinking instant coffee all night and arguing passionately about ideas. We also talked about our ambitions. Bill always used to say: 'I don't care what job I do, so long as it helps to make this crazy old world of ours a better place.'

I confessed that I burned to be a humorous columnist on a conservative Sunday newspaper. 'This ambition rules my life,' I said fiercely. 'I'll do anything to get that job, whatever the cost, whoever else gets hurt.'

'Hey, hey, lighten up, Oliver,' Bill would say.

Of the others, Honkers Chuffington said he wanted to be 'some kind of spy', while Willie Rees-Mogg (Old Couch Potato, as we called him) was looking for an opening in show business. Jeffrey Archer was the most withdrawn; having already become the youngest-ever Fellow of All Souls, he seemed to have run out of ambition.

Bill Clinton had his problems, too. I remember he once came to me in a terrible state. 'I believe I may have passively smoked marijuana,' he said. 'While I was jogging in Christ Church Meadow I think I ran within twenty yards of someone who was smoking a joint.' It was with some difficulty that I dissuaded him from reporting himself to the proctors.

Yes, I do remember him being less than honest on one occasion. He rowed in the Oxford crew in the boat race under a false name. Bill fractured his wrist on a clash of oars while shooting Barnes Bridge, but even so, Oxford won by twenty-seven lengths: Bill swore me to secrecy but said he used the name of a fellow undergraduate who wanted to be a Tory MP 'just to give him a start in life'.

One day Honkers Chuffington and I went down to London for a lunch of the Absolutely Ghastly Society, and then, rather fuddled, went on to a Vietnam war demonstration in Grosvenor Square. In the course of events old Chuffington's cigar happened to ignite the American flag I was carrying. Suddenly, Bill Clinton pushed his way through the crowd and snatched the flag from me. 'Are you crazy?' he cried. 'What about your ambition to be a humorous columnist on a conservative Sunday newspaper? This could really blow your chances. The place is crawling with *Daily Telegraph* photographers.' At that moment Honkers Chuffington took a snap of Bill holding the smouldering flag.

My last memory of Bill was of him standing next to me and watching the sun rise over Magdalen Tower. Bill was playing his saxophone. It was a blue note, full of yearning, but also hope somehow. His sparrow, Abe, was perched on his shoulder.

'I guess all I want in this life,' he told me, 'is to marry a good woman who spells her first name in an unusual way.'

65

Exit blushing from bank

'I know a bank,' says Oberon to Puck in *A Midsummer Night's Dream*. It is pretty clear to me that in this speech Oberon is referring to the National Westminster. I have to admit that not much wild thyme blows on my particular branch and perhaps I have been too preoccupied while queuing to notice the oxslips and the nodding violets, but there could be a simple explanation. Oberon was probably overdrawn. He was overstating the charms of the Woodland branch of NatWest to flatter the manager and ward off reproachful letters. A wise move.

True to its theatrical traditions, the wise, splendidly altruistic, endlessly and nobly patient National Westminster Bank is again sponsoring a tour of Britain by the Royal Shakespeare Company, starting in Scunthorpe on Tuesday and going on for fifteen weeks. I am sure my own manager must have had a hand in this imaginative scheme.

The connection between banking and the theatre is plain to see. A visit to the bank is, after all, a dramatic occasion. The villain of the piece is easily identified: he is the man with the large canvas bag containing £486.35 in five and ten pence pieces which he is about to pay in, along with eighteen assorted cheques which he wishes to be credited to a variety of accounts. He also has a very long soliloquy which he delivers in order to slow up the action of the drama and build up the suspense in the queue.

The young hero waits with pounding heart and demurely lowered eyes (in case the manager walks past) in a state of obvious agitation. At last he is face to face with the teller and everybody is watching him. Surreptitiously he slides a piece of paper towards her and for an instant their eyes meet through

186

the bullet-proof glass which so cruelly separates them, like Pyramus and Thisby. 'How would you like it?' she breathes. 'Four fives and five ones,' he replies, and even though he is choking with emotion he gets the metre just right. Exit pursued by a glare.

Then there is often the street theatre outside the bank. It is the well-known Rejection Scene: the hero has placed his plastic card in the cash dispenser and after some moments of thoughtful whirring the machine has refused to pay out. The hero turns to the three disbelieving customers in the queue behind him and gives a brave laugh. 'I can't understand it,' he blurts out. 'There must be something wrong with the machine . . . Maybe I got my number wrong . . . I mean, it's not as if . . .' The three people in the queue, confident of their own credit, watch him running off down the street.

The other clearing banks should follow NatWest's fine example and go into the theatrical business even more seriously. It could transform life in the West End.

The timing of the performances will have to be changed, of course, because the curtain must come down promptly at 3.30 p.m. As we wait outside the theatre we can see that the critics enjoyed the show. Just look at the billboards. 'The interest never flags' – *Investor's Chronicle*. 'All the cast deserve unlimited credit' – *The Economist*.

We stand in the queue waiting for the green arrow to flash and the discreet 'ping' to sound, telling us that it is our turn at the box office. 'How would you like the seats?' the girl asks. 'Two stalls and three dress circles,' we reply.

As we linger in the foyer we take the opportunity to study the theatre programme. It is printed by a computer and the information it contains is limited and unembroidered. When we read the programme we gasp: 'Good heavens! I'm sure there ought to be more actors in the cast than this! I can't understand where they all go.'

We are interrupted by the ringing of a bell and an announcement by the house manager over the public address system: 'Dear Sir, further to my earlier announcement that the curtain will rise in three minutes, I note that you still have not taken your seat in the auditorium. I should be grateful if you would look in to see me as soon as possible to discuss the situation as the performance is about to begin.'

The play is a new farce entitled *Do You Have an Arrangement?* The first act is a hilarious parade of high hopes and sudden disappointments, repentance, reckless promises, surprise entrances and unexpected outgoings.

At the interval a blind is lowered from the proscenium arch saying 'Position Closed' and we join the orderly stampede to the stalls bar. Inevitably, ahead of us there is a man who is ordering an immensely complicated round of drinks which he is going to pay for in ten pence and five pence pieces from the large canvas bag he is carrying. We finger our change nervously, wondering if there are sufficient funds to cover the gin and tonic transaction and we make desultory intellectual conversation about the show. 'Do you think the author is trying to make a Statement?'

In act two the whole complicated business is resolved and we see that the plot turns on a case of mistaken identity and a misplaced decimal point. The members of the cast take a curtain call and we give them an enthusiastic standing order.

'It does you good to get out occasionally,' we say as we leave the theatre. 'Still, it's an expensive business. I am going to have to pop up the street and get some money from the Arts Council cash dispenser.'

66

Platform performance

This is a tremendously exciting time in the London theatre and I am thrilled to be creatively involved. You probably saw in yesterday's paper that Network SouthEast had announced that British Rail was joining with West End Theatres to offer combined ticket-travel packages with discounts.

This means the coming together of two art forms in which the British excel – the theatre and commuting. I have wasted no time in mounting a brand new production of Shakespeare's comedy *All's Well That Terminates Here*. It breaks new ground, both theatrically and in railway terms, which is why we call it Avant Guard.

As a theatre director, I like to create an atmosphere of danger, and that is why I have chosen for the part of Bertram a promising young actor who lives in Southend and catches a train to Fenchurch Street every evening. Sometimes he does not arrive at the theatre until halfway through Act 1, Scene 3 and the other members of the cast have to improvise until then.

The 'buzz' at the theatre is wonderful. It must be very like the atmosphere at the Globe in Elizabethan times. The excitement is almost tangible, from the moment of the announcement in the foyer: 'Ladies and gentlemen, please take your seats; the curtain will rise in 35 minutes.'

There is no rush to the bar in the interval, because throughout the evening a woman with a trolley patrols the aisles calling out: 'Any drinks or light refreshments?'

Then there are a few diversions when the party from Haywards Heath, booked for rows E to J, have to have the plot explained to them and they, in turn, explain that they are late because of a points failure at East Croydon.

The interaction between the audience and cast owes a great

deal to Brecht and also a considerable amount to the 7.56 from Tunbridge Wells to Charing Cross. As the play proceeds, a ticket inspector moves among the people in the stalls and the dress circle. From time to time, you hear him say: 'I'm sorry, madam, but this ticket is not valid for Act 3, Scene 4.' There was an interesting twist in the plot last week when it was discovered that the girl who plays Helena was doing so on an expired season ticket.

The splendid thing about this marriage of the theatre and rail is that it has also had a good effect on Network SouthEast. When there are loudspeaker announcements of delays you will be impressed by the greatly improved enunciation. I have also noticed that train drivers now tend to refer to the journey from West Norwood to Clapham Junction as The Pre-London Run, and a lot of gushing and kissing takes place when they arrive on time. There is a BR employee at Victoria who, as people give him their tickets on leaving the platform, says: 'Thank you, thank you. Everybody has been simply marvellous.'

And there is a member of the station staff at Orpington who gave such a moving and convincing performance last Wednesday when he said he regretted the inconvenience caused by the non-arrival of the 8.17 that he reduced many hardened commuters to tears and had to take nine curtain calls.

He was 'discovered' by a theatrical impresario who happened to be there at the time because he had missed his connection to Hastings. Later in the year he is to star at Chichester in a production of *A Man for All Season Tickets*.

67

Time to call a halt to conductors' glory days

The row about the playing of 'Land of Hope and Glory' on the Last Night of the Proms raises wider, more important issues. It brings home to us the fundamentally reactionary structure of the traditional symphony orchestra.

You have only to consider the role of the conductor. Here is an unelected individual with complete discretionary powers to decide if a particular passage should be played mezzoforte or fortissimo. It is he who rules, without prior consultation, that the violas should come in at the beginning of the forty-seventh bar.

With an imperiously dismissive gesture, he brings the first movement to a close, yet no one has the courage to ask him if he has a mandate for this. At the end of the concert he gets almost all the glory. He may permit the members of the orchestra to rise to their feet, adopt a hangdog expression and give a perfunctory bow, but that is all.

This sort of thing would not be tolerated in any other area of society. That is why I have teamed up with some progressive elements in the musical world to set up COD – the Campaign for Orchestral Democracy. We are already pressing for more women conductors and for free elections in all orchestras. There is also a case for having a committee of six or seven conductors who, with the consent of the orchestra, would jointly put into effect the wishes of all sections.

As we see it, the conductor's baton and his podium are simply the trappings of an outdated dictatorship. These should be abolished and he (or she) should be seated with the rest of the orchestra.

It is also our view that important policy decisions about whether a passage is to be played *presto* or *adagio* should not be taken without the full, democratically arrived at, consent of the whole orchestra, and that a conductor could be removed from office at any point in a symphony on a two-thirds majority vote in the strings section.

The seating arrangements in orchestras have also had the effect of preserving an outmoded musical class structure. Under our scheme, flautists would be able to mix freely with cellists, and the trombonists could associate on equal terms with the oboists. It is hoped that they would also exchange instruments during the course of the symphony so that each musician would feel that he had a full part to play in a more meaningful composer–audience relationship.

The power to choose the music to be played at a concert is now concentrated in too few hands. This is where the audience could come in. They could vote, by a system of proportional representation, on what they would like to hear.

68

All alone in the theatre of war

The shortage of American tourists in London, we are told, has had a depressing effect on the West End theatre. Apparently you can now easily get tickets for just about any show in town – which rather spoils the pleasure of the whole business. One of the joys of going to the theatre is swanking about how you have been able, through special influence, to acquire two stalls seats for *Okehampton!* that exciting new musical about early closing day in a Devon market town.

You may think it inconsiderate of the Americans to stop supporting our theatre and to leave it to us, but this may, in the end, be a good thing.

There is a wealth of dramatic potential in this situation. It has certainly stimulated me and I have written a play about it. Three actors hang around on stage for a couple of hours and engage in seemingly pointless conversation as they wonder if an American tourist will ever come into the theatre and watch them. It is called *Waiting for Morton F. Godot*.

I have also written a rather more *avant garde* piece which is set in a West End theatre box-office. In the first act the phone rings continuously and is ignored by the box office manageress. Nothing else happens. In the second act the phone does not ring at all, the tension builds up and the manageress gradually goes mad.

In these hard times when I go to the theatre I make a point of asking for a seat behind a pillar. You do not want to feel too exposed and self-conscious in those wide open spaces in the stalls. You do not want to feel that the leading lady is addressing her poignant all-men-are-absolute-rotters speech directly at you. The extraordinary thing is that, even if there is only one other person there, right at the other end of the auditorium, he still manages to step on your foot when he takes his place.

The sparseness of audiences has also led to some exciting new experiments in theatre. The other night I was watching a performance of *Hamlet* when one of the seven other people in the audience stood up and said: 'We need two volunteers from the stage to come and join us in the stalls. Come on, don't be shy.'

Eventually the girl who was Ophelia and the chap who played Laertes came down, blushing and giggling. Actually, I think they had a marvellous time joining in enthusiastically with the applause and being taught the basic techniques of dropping their programmes on the floor and rushing to the bar in the interval.

As a matter of fact there is still one American tourist in London, and he is still conscientiously going to all the theatres. In fact he has become something of a celebrity, with chat show hosts falling over each other to get him on their programmes. His name is Wilbur Westbury and I was lucky enough to get an interview with him last week.

'Mr Westbury,' I said, 'you have been coming to the London theatre for many years now. When did your theatre-going career actually begin?'

'I started out about fifteen years ago. In those days I just played the part of the British stereotype of the American tourist with the 'loud' whispers in the dress circle. You know the sort of line – "It's an allegory, Martha. An *allegory*, for heaven's sake." I had quite a lot of parts like that.'

'One of your memorable lines, of course, was delivered across fourteen rows of seats at the Aldwych theatre, I recall,' I said. 'That was when you said, "No, honey, Cesario is really a dame dressed up as a man.' They did a lot of that sort of thing when Shakespeare was on the 'throne.'" Was that a demanding role?'

'It was pretty corny stuff,' Mr Westbury said. 'But the Brits seemed to like it.'

'Now you have been very busy with your play-going in recent weeks. And you have become something of a tourist attraction yourself. And you have been very busy.'

'Yes, sometimes I have to leave after the first scene in one play and then rush off to be a latecomer at another theatre, then dashing across town for the curtain calls at the National. It's not all glamour being London's only tourist, you know. Of course, it is nice to have the Changing of the Guard performed for your convenience in your own hotel suite, and you get excellent in-flight attention if you are the only passenger on a transatlantic jumbo, but in the end it is just a question of showing up at the theatre on the night and doing your stuff.'

69

Received any haste mail recently?

Caroline. Just a quick note to say I have left a note for the wine people to push the Rioja through the cat-flap. Have told washing-up machine maintenance engineer to try again on Thursday week, stressing a.m. Did you see report of National Family Trust? Says most family communication these days consists more of hastily scribbled notes than face-to-face conversation. Families lead separate lives under the same roof. V. intrstng. Must dash. Things at office getting v. hairy. Prendergast brooding. Love, Jasper.

J. Sorry I missed you. Fiona's oboe on the blink again and *chaos* at keep-fit class when Mrs W got over-ambitious on rowing machine. Can you arrange to have pizzas biked over? In haste, C.

C. Pizzas non-event, I'm afraid. Your note so hastily scribbled that I thought it said 'pince-nez'. Optician had no biking facilities, but made an appointment for you for a fortnight on Monday. Have to zoom. Atmosphere in office brooding, Prendergast hairy. Love J.

J. Please cancel opticians' appointment. Busy with bypass protest meeting fortnight next Monday. And no particular desire for pince-nez. Cat upset about Rioja blockage in cat-flap and left 'message' in sitting room. Love C.

C. Why no hastily scribbled note today?

J. My fault. Scrawled note in rush but left it for milkman by mistake.

C. Touched that you remembered our wedding anniversary. Got your nice message on the telephone-answering machine. Did you see mine in personal column of the *Soya Trade Journal*? Don't forget to set the video to record *Inspector Morse*. How is your new job? P is now hairy and brooding.

J. Thought your message was in the personal column of the *Architectural Review*. Was rather thrown by use of nickname. 'Scratty-poo'. All now explained. Found a dashed-off letter in fridge today from 'N'. Who is N? Love C.

C. Think N must be the milkman. He was very touched by your hastily scribbled note the other day. Pity we did not get a chance to have more than a hurriedly gabbled conversation at the Wilkinsons' dinner party last night. Loved your new hairstyle, hated the chilli con carne. Must fly – showdown with Prendergast.

Jasper. I did not go to the Wilkinsons' dinner party. Attending Fiona's school concert. Didn't you get my hasty note? Caroline.

C. Oops! While speed-reading your lightning missive, I must have got the meaning wrong. Person I was talking to at dinner party was probably our au pair, W (or is it D?). By the way, have you seen the laboriously penned communication from Mrs B? Who is Mrs B? Love J.

J. Mrs B is the cleaning lady. She has resigned because of what the cat did in the sitting room and because of the screwed up pieces of paper all over the house. She was giving us a piece of her mind. Love, C.

Caroline. Found this card from the washing-up machine maintenance engineer through the letterbox. He called, as arranged, but we were out. Those odd people at number 32 say our cat has moved in with them and do we want it back? The laundry man has left a hastily scribbled bill and there is a registered package they have tried to deliver four times which can now be collected from the post office. Can you cope? Things a bit hectic. Must go and compose a lengthy carefully worded memo re *l'affaire Prendergast*. Love, J.

J. Extraordinary news! It seems that Mrs B, the cleaning lady, has been conducting a passionate correspondence with the milkman. Found a huge bundle of flowery love letters stuffed in the washing-up machine. They go on for *pages*! That is the reason she resigned. They are planning to set up a little creative writing school together in Tiverton. Isn't that romantic? Must skedaddle. Lucy is having another crisis with her Aga. Love, C.

Caroline. I have a hastily scribbled confession to make. I

resigned from my job three weeks ago. Since then I have been hiding in the airing cupboard, leaving you notes. All that stuff about the brooding Prendergast was made up. I was wondering if we could possibly meet up? Slip a note under the airing cupboard door if you agree. Love, J.

Dear Jasper. It would be lovely to meet. After all this time I feel strangely shy. You don't think we are being too hasty, do you? Love, Caroline.

October

70

Cry God for Harry, if it's all right by you

Henry V had a good week. After being portrayed on film by Kenneth Branagh, his Agincourt speech was ringingly quoted by Kenneth Baker at the Tory Party Conference. Something else that was said at the conference has moved me to make some adjustments to the play.

Sir Geoffrey Howe told a fringe meeting that it was time for the Conservatives to become a 'listening' party to match the mood of Britain. This is the new fad of the eager-to-please. After that listening bank, we have the Government graciously paying heed.

My new production of *Henry V* matches the national mood and gives the king a new 'softer' image. He is seen as a monarch who combines qualities of leadership with a knowledge of the principles of enlightened management.

The revised Agincourt scene gives some of the flavour. A crowd of assorted lords and soldiers are hanging around nervously in the camp on the eve of the battle. Henry enters with a folder and a diffident smile and sits down placing his fingertips together thoughtfully.

'Was there something you wanted to say?' the Earl of Westmorland inquires.

'No, no. You chaps carry on. I'm just here to listen.'

'We thought perhaps you might want to make a rousing speech. Rallying the troops, a call to arms. We thought you might be planning a bit of morale-boosting.'

'Oh, you don't want to hear me banging on in some lengthy monologue about we few, we happy few, we band of brothers and all that. I'd be much more interested to have your views about the difficult task facing us.'

'Some of the lads were saying a minute ago that he which

hath no stomach to this fight, let him depart,' one of the soldiers mentions haltingly.

'This is very good. Now we are getting a dialogue going. The ideas are bouncing about. I like this.'

Another soldier raises his hand. 'Excuse me, Mr Fifth . . .'

'Call me Henry, please. After all, I've met a lot of you fellows in the canteen.'

'Excuse me, Mr Henry. I noticed that this day is called the feast of Crispian. I was wondering if this could be relevant in any way, shape or form.'

'Well, I had just thought of this day as the commencement of Week 27. But if a majority of the men would like to call it the feast of Crispian I would be more than happy to go along with this and have the day redesignated.'

'Do you think it will be all right if he that outlives this day and comes safe home will stand a tip-toe when this day is named and rouse him at the name of Crispian?'

'Well, obviously I am not in a position to forecast the outcome of the battle at this stage. And as for standing a tip-toe, that is a decision that must be left to the individual. All I can say is that I am anxious to keep the lines of communication open and if at any time any man wants to come and talk about his problems or even to strip his sleeve and show his scars, I am available. That is what I am here for, after all. My tent flap is always open.'

Henry looks inquiringly round the crowd of soldiers. 'Anybody else got any points they'd like to raise at this juncture? This is the moment to speak. We have got to think of ourselves as a team, all making our contribution. Surely, one of you chaps lurking at the back has got something he'd like to get off his chest.'

An old soldier is pushed forward by his companions. 'There's a rumour going round the camp,' he says, 'that gentlemen in England now a-bed shall think themselves accurs'd they were not here.'

'I'm very glad you brought this to my attention. I would be most distressed if any group were to feel itself accurs'd, left out or in any way alienated by what we are doing here today.'

He stands up and starts pacing. Soon he reaches a decision.

'It seems to me that what we urgently need is closer liaison between ourselves and the gentlemen in England now a-bed. I think we should set up the appropriate machinery and until this is done it would be better to suspend our Agincourt operation.'

The soldiers disperse. Henry draws his sword, brandishes it heroically and declaims: 'This has been extremely helpful. I think it would be a good idea to hold these talks on a regular basis.'

71

Looks like a case for the Mould Bill

Having the odd forty minutes to spare last week I decided to dash off a new TV police thriller series. After ten minutes the going was getting tough, then, by chance, I caught sight of the item in the paper about the Prince of Wales defending the pongy varieties of French cheeses and some other 'gloriously unhygienic' foods mankind has created against the pettifogging EC bureaucrats and the 'bacteriological police'.

What a great concept! Bacteriological police. I was on to my agent in a flash with the outline for a new series called *Bacillus*. This is the story of Lieut Joe Bacillus of the Germicide Squad in the LAPD. He wears an immaculately clean raincoat and has a sidekick called Mike Microbe. The first episode is action-packed. Joe Bacillus gets a call to go to a downtown surf 'n' turf diner where unhygienic activity is reported to be taking place. 'Mind how you go, Joe,' the precinct captain tells him. 'This guy could do something desperate like sneezing without putting his handkerchief in front of his mouth.'

Joe Bacillus walks towards the diner and calls through a loud-hailer: 'OK. We've got the place surrounded, so come on out with your hands washed.'

I also wrote a gritty series set in London, about a team of coppers who are trying to bust a gang that has been leaving hairy green mould on the top of tens of thousands of jars of home-made raspberry jam. It is called *The Fuzz*.

Since the Prince of Wales made his sensible observations about cheeses and hygiene in Paris, I thought I should add my own bacteriological episodes to *Maigret*:

We find Chief Inspector Maigret seated at his desk at the Quai des Orfèvres looking impatiently through paperwork.

There is a knock at the door. 'Come in,' he growls. It is his assistants, Boursin and Roquefort.

'A body has been found in the Seine, chief,' says Boursin. 'Just by the Pont l'Evêque. It is Gaston, the old accordion-restorer. They think it is food poisoning and *moules* are suspected.'

'Right,' says Maigret. 'Boursin, you go and have a Kronenbourg and half a dozen *pieds de porc* at the café opposite and keep an eye on the apartment block, and, Roquefort, you go and ask a few questions and see if you can sniff anything out.'

'And what are you going to do, chief?'

'I am going to have one more attempt at lighting my pipe, then I will stroll moodily home, eat a *cassoulet* and half-listen as Mme Maigret tells me I work too hard.'

Two days later, the faithful underlings return. 'What news?' growls the Chief Inspector. Boursin tells him about the occupants of the apartment block where Gaston, the old accordion-restorer, used to live. 'On the first floor there is the Widow Camembert. Nothing really suspiciously unhygienic about her, except that she wipes her spoon on her cardigan before she eats her *potage bonne femme*.'

Roquefort adds his own report. 'On the top floor there is an English *milord* who has a well-hung pheasant next to the tweed suit in his wardrobe. Then there is Mademoiselle Salmonella, a *fille de joie*. I thought you might like to have a scene with her later on, full of pregnant pauses and ruminative puffs. The one I have my doubts about is Monsieur André, the one-legged beret-shaper in the basement. He was very keen that I should not observe that his *quenelle de brochet* was past its best-before date.'

'I think it is time we went to have a little word with our friend the beret-shaper,' says Maigret. 'We might take some of that *quenelle* away for the examining magistrate to examine.'

They troop round to the apartment block, narrowly avoiding being run over by seventeen elderly Citroëns. As they arrive at the apartment, André is preparing his lunch. 'Ah, the famous Chief Inspector Maigret,' he says. 'To what do I owe the pleasure?' Maigret looks inscrutable; some ash from his pipe falls onto the lapel of his raincoat and he carelessly brushes it away so that it falls into the *bouillabaisse*. Everyone now realises that he is the Paris food-polluter. He is arrested and taken away.

'Oh well, there's always one rotten apple in the barrel,' says Roquefort.

'Sounds delicious,' Boursin replies.

72

Luminaries of the bulb business

Pritchett's Second Law states: 'Any light bulb, when shaken, will rattle.' (This followed my First Law, which states: 'All milk, when sniffed, smells "off".')

73

The fish knives are out

'Who is the turbot?' He stood there, appraising us carefully, apparently searching for fish-like characteristics in our features. At last, the scales, as it were, dropped from my eyes.

'Ah, my companion is having the fish,' I replied. The waiter, having made the wrong guess, moved round the table and rearranged my companion's cutlery noisily. It was a message of reassurance. Even though we had just about forgotten what we had ordered it was good to know there was still some record of it in the kitchens.

Incidentally, I like this word 'companion.' Restaurant critics in newspapers and magazines always seem to use it, discreetly preserving the anonymity of the person across the table. It carries the suggestion of romance, of illicit meetings, of trysts. I find myself forgetting about the subject matter of the restaurant review and speculating about the relationship between the companion and the critic.

That would make a more interesting gastronomic guide – 'My companion spoke highly of the lightness of the pastry cases and was impressed by the texture of the cucumber sauce, but commented unfavourably on my shirt and went on to declare that she found my general attitude to life "disappointingly soggy." Resisting the temptations of the adventurous cheeseboard and the widely-acclaimed sweet trolley, she abruptly left the restaurant saying she now realised she had made the wrong choice and never wanted to see me again.'

Anyway, to pass the time before the turbot arrived, I made efforts to call the waiter over to the table once more. He circled for a while, then approached, right shoulder first, wary, dreading some outlandish demand, like another bread roll to sustain us.

'The Society for American Cuisine is offering prizes totalling £35,000 in a competition for an essay defining the virtues of the perfect waiter,' I said. 'As a matter of fact, I have managed to knock off the first seventeen pages of mine while waiting for the avocado pear. Perhaps you might like to have a look at it.'

'And perhaps you would like to read the manuscript of my satirical novel about restaurant customers, sir,' the waiter said. 'Is is called *From Here To Gratuity* and contains many sharp observations and penetrating insights.'

'I never read manuscripts on an empty stomach,' I replied.

As he returned to the kitchens he made the swing doors swing with magnificent eloquence. On the other side there was a shout like scalding water.

'It looks as though we can kiss goodbye to the turbot,' my companion observed.

'In this country, I think it is the self-image of the customer, not the waiter, which needs attention,' I said. 'This is one of the main themes of my essay for this competition. All that decision-making over the menu makes us so vulnerable. That is when we need to build up a good head of esteem. The waiter whispers today's special to you like a confidence, but you know he is telling everybody else as well. When you resist his suggestion you wonder how you are going to win back his friendship. He looks deadpan when he takes your order and you suspect he despises your choice.'

Our waiter was now paying exaggerated attention to the money brokers at the next table.

'Not that you want too much fuss,' I went on. 'There is a passage in my essay called The Acceptable Level of Hovering. And you do not want effusiveness. There is a waiter at an Italian restaurant I no longer dare to go to whose histrionics are even more preposterous than his pepper-mill. When I ask for spinach to go with my veal escalope he throws his arms in the air and shouts "wonderful!" as if I had just discovered an inspired combination of flavour and texture that nobody else had ever thought of before.'

My companion picked up her glass and joined the money brokers at their table.

'The thing is,' I said to the wine waiter who happened to

be passing, 'it is not just the waiters who look like retired second violin players or dinner-jacketed boxers who are intimidating. It is just as bad when you go to these modern places and are served by young people in white shirts, with tiny aprons and hips slender as asparagus. They describe in detail every *nouvelle cuisine* item on the menu. And the thing about *nouvelle cuisine* is that it takes less time to eat it than it does to describe it.'

The wine waiter put on his hat and coat and went home.

'I do not mind being kept waiting, actually,' I said to the sweet trolley. 'This is another theme of my essay. One of the qualities of the perfect waiter is that he should also provide food for thought. You need to ponder about the politics among the waiters, the pecking order, the secret hostilities. You know that you are seeing only half the show, that something more interesting is going on behind the scenes. What dramas are occurring behind that swing door?' The raspberry mousse shuddered and seemed to sag.

I leaned across to my companion at the next table. 'You always notice how, when they come out of the kitchen, they look so emotionally fulfilled,' said. 'I long to know what goes on in there. On the other hand, I have sometimes thought that if I did get up and sneak in there all I would find is a deep freeze, a microwave cooker and a tape recorder playing the sound effects of a culinary melodrama.'

As my companion left the restaurant with the money brokers I called after her: 'How did you find your meal?'

'Somewhat over-opinionated,' she said.

'And the essay?'

'Overdone.'

74

An everyday story of ostrich folk

It has been a quiet week down here in Utter Wittering. Now the nights are drawing in, most of the villagers stay at home to listen to *The Archers* and don't venture out after that. You can lie in bed and listen to the sounds of the countryside, like the rasping breathless noise and the pad pad pad as one of old Ned Silage's escaping ostriches comes racing down the village street.

These ostriches are becoming a bit of a problem. As you know, ostrich farming is developing in this country – the meat is supposed to have a 'gamey' venison taste – so the RSPCA has laid down forty-six guidelines for protecting their welfare. Of course, this is woefully inadequate.

In Utter Wittering ostriches are a traffic hazard when they escape. At full stretch, they can run at 40 m.p.h. Now, we don't have a speed limit in the village and there's no street lighting. We've been on to the county council about this, but to no avail.

So, you can imagine what can happen if you get an ostrich roaring down the street after dark at 40 m.p.h. in the direction of the caravan park and it collides with a couple of Bill Bale's wild boar, which in spite of also having a gamey venison taste, do not get on well with ostriches. That blind corner by the dairy where they process the moose cheese is an accident black spot ostrich-wise. I've written to the parish council about it, but they haven't replied. They're sticking their heads in the sand over this one, I'm afraid.

Now, your average ostrich has a pretty vicious kick, while a wild boar can turn quite nasty when cornered – for example when backed into the lay-by where the bottle bank is. As far as I know, the RSPCA has not yet indicated what position it would take on a confrontation between an ostrich and a wild boar.

This situation has the makings of a major disaster. These dark mornings the big delicatessen lorries roll into the village very early. They might have to swerve to avoid the moose herd being brought in for milking, then be distracted by Christopher Booker (who could be in the village to check on the petty hygiene regulations in the wild boar sausage-smoking plant) and come slap up against an ostrich engaged in kung fu-style mortal combat.

All this could easily set off a stampede in old Jethro Barley's herd of red deer, which, as well as having a gamey venison taste, are of a nervous disposition.

Between you and me, I believe it is Mrs Maize who lets the ostriches out. Her family has had a feud with Ned Silage for the past six years. They say Ned took the side of Billy Kale when his armadillo (gamey) got shot for worrying her broody pelicans (sort of tuna flavour) when Billy swore blind it wasn't the armadillo, but an escaped rogue wildebeest which had been spotted in the area on several occasions and had, on the night before, been seen in the fifteen acre radicchio meadow.

It didn't help when Ned's younger son got Mrs Maize's niece into trouble, then ran off to the big city to set up his hand-loomed horse-blanket business and the niece had to support the twins by working nights in the moose cheese factory. That was the year Sam Binder shot himself after the dill harvest failed and Bill Bale got a poisoned foot after he was bitten by a coypu.

Funny thing, we were discussing coypu in the pub the other day over a ploughman's lunch (coarse free-range giraffe pâté in a roll, topped with locally-grown sesame seeds) and we were remembering mink. Now, if ostriches are going to escape and 'go native' like coypu and mink we could be in serious trouble. I'm thinking about footpaths. Suppose you are using a properly designated footpath and an ostrich leaps out of the hedge and kicks you on the jaw. Who is liable?

The RSPCA says ostriches are gregarious. So, we're really talking about packs of ostriches roaming free. If nothing is done, we'll soon have the problem of the urban ostrich. You will get twenty or thirty at a time racing round housing estates, scavenging for food and kicking over residents and dustbins. They will start terrorising the local alsations and rottweilers and they will remove manhole covers so that they can stick their heads below ground.

Nowadays I lie awake at night listening to the ostriches padding past and I dream up guidelines.

75

They also read who sit and wait

The old cliché about *Punch* in dentists' waiting rooms has always been rather unfair to the magazine and also fails to do justice to the wealth of reading material that dentists provide. Usually, when you go to the dentist, you find that he has kindly left out his old left-over copies of *Yachting World* and *The Extremely Rich Person's Guide to Antique Collecting*.

These are the sort of thing that give one a nasty throbbing ache of envy in the wallet. There is worse to come. You pick up another magazine and you discover it is something like *Hang-Gliding for Daredevils*. Do you really want to surrender your gums to someone who gets a kick out of living dangerously?

I sometimes make the mistake of trying to draw a psychological portrait of the dentist, based on the magazines he has put on display. I get a certain sense of unease if I discover he is a regular subscriber to *Which Rottweiler?*. I'd like to see evidence of a steadier, if duller, sort of character – like a well-thumbed copy of *Cactus World* or *The Practical Caravanner*.

There are other things to read – like the dentist's framed certificates. There they are, scrolled and sealed and certifying that the dentist has been commended for his capping and bridge-work. I am always rather wary of getting up and walking across to read these more closely, because the dentist may come out of his room at that moment, suspect that I am doubting his credentials and then express his hurt feelings in the only way he knows how.

Or you can admire the pictures on the wall. There is an inappropriately chocolate-boxish portrait of a kitten and a romanticised scene of a cool Scottish mountain stream. There is also a garish diagram of all the dreadful things plaque can do and a picture of a cross-section of a tooth which appears to contain far too many nerves for my liking.

Meanwhile the dentist himself (or herself) is probably trying to manipulate our mood through magazines. Those 1969 copies of *Country Life* are put there for a purpose. They are supposed to soothe us, I imagine. They are obviously an improvement on the *National Enquirer* which would be bound to have some story like 'Woman Has Hamster Foetus Implanted in Molar'. Or perhaps 'My Fillings Picked Up Signals from Mars'.

The 1969 issues of *Country Life* are there to lure us into comfortable daydreams. We turn to the property advertisements and imagine ourselves buying that castle in Fife or that Georgian mansion in Berkshire with 2,500 acres of very green parkland and (thank goodness) ample stabling. At 1969 property prices, these dreams seem slightly less preposterously out of reach. That is why the cunning dentists purposely display the out-of-date copies.

Who tears the covers off all the magazines and removes certain pages? I used to believe that this was the work of a single, obsessive person with a grudge. Perhaps he was an embittered *Punch* cartoonist, a man who had been forced by his creditors to sell off his castle in Fife and advertise it in *Country Life*, or, more likely, a tragic young fellow whose fiancée eloped with a dentist after being dazzled by his certificates for capping and bridge-work. In revenge, he went round all the dentists' waiting rooms in the country mutilating the magazines.

I now realise I was wrong. The truth is much more interesting – it is the *dentists themselves* who tear the pages out. They don't want us to settle down for a good read in the waiting room. Imagine what would happen. The dentist would emerge from his room saying he was ready to tackle your root canal and he would find you immersed in the 1969 *Country Life*. 'Can't come just yet,' you would say. 'I'm just finishing this fascinating article about ducking stools in Dorset.' Or: 'I'll be with you in a couple of minutes – just as soon as I have found out if sedge warblers mate for life.'

There could be a market here, perhaps, for a collection of

short stories designed to be read in dentists' waiting rooms and capturing the overriding emotion in these places which is a furtive sense of injustice. Here is the opening of my first short story, entitled *The Lady-in-Waiting*:

'Flora Caries, the dark-eyed young horsewoman, stood in the ample stabling at Novocaine Castle, in Fife, when the handsome Laird arrived carrying his favourite hunting sedge warbler on his wrist. He ignored Flora and beckoned to Flossie Dental, the flighty redhead, to follow him into the castle. It was so unfair, Flora thought. She had been waiting for far longer than Flossie Dental who had flounced in only two minutes ago . . .'

76

The spy who came in from the blurb

The instructions, written on the back of an old seed catalogue and pushed under my door, were precise. I was to go to a particular hamburger joint in the less-good part of Wimbledon at nine o'clock the following Thursday morning, order a quarter-pounder with cheese and wait to be contacted.

It was a dismal, drizzly day. I watched the raindrops smear their way down the window of the hamburger joint and I toyed fretfully with the sachet of ketchup. Outside, old tabloid newspapers blew along the pavement and wrapped themselves round the ankles of people hurrying to the Tube. A mongrel dog cringed by the pillar-box; two men were clamping an illegally-parked car. My sesame bun sagged.

After an hour-and-a-half two men came in. The taller one wore an Old Haileyburian tie, slightly stained at the tip. The other man had very small feet and a complexion the colour of the *Financial Times*.

They bought a banana milkshake and two straws. As they drank together their eyes never left me. I had an uneasy feeling I had seen them somewhere before.

Outside, the last of the autumn leaves gave up hope and flopped to the ground and a schoolgirl kicked the cringing dog. I heard the gurgle as the men finished their milk-shake and the next moment they were beside me. The tall one lifted the top off my sesame bun, picked up the meagre slice of pickled cucumber and chewed it slowly.

'We have been watching you for some time,' he said. 'Following your progress. Undistinguished career at undistinguished university. Humdrum job. Routine existence. No close friendships. Failed in application for TSB shares.'

'You are ideal,' said the man with small feet. 'Just the chap

217

we want. We have a little project for you. Rather secret. We want you to write a book.'

It was then that I realised who they were. I had caught an occasional glimpse of them in Bloomsbury from the top of a 24 bus. They were Faber and Faber.

Faber nodded to Faber who pushed a contract in front of me. 'Quite simple. Standard contract. One thousand pounds advance, one thousand pounds on delivery. We keep the Australian rights.'

'What is the book about?' I asked.

'Your life in MI5.'

'But I am not even a member,' I protested.

'We can get you in,' said Faber smirking at Faber. 'You will also be attending MI5 Creative Writing classes every Monday evening.'

They left. I gave them ten minutes' start then made my way along the street. I do not know exactly what happened then. There was a shout, the roar of a car's engine, then everything seemed to be spinning – the shoppers, the cringing mongrel, a postman, old newspapers and heavy, soggy leaves. I found myself lying on the ground, bruised but not badly hurt. A black car swerved off the pavement and sped away. I caught a glimpse of the driver. It was a woman with long dark hair and a scarlet silk scarf. I was almost certain I recognised her as a senior non-fiction editor at Gollancz.

I spent the rest of the day walking in the rain in Hyde Park trying to clear my thoughts. It was after nine o'clock in the evening when I returned to my bedsitter. I climbed the worn stairs that smelled of stale gravy and musty gas bills and on the second landing a bulky figure brushed past me in the darkness. When I got to my room I knew at once that I had had a visitor. My copy of *Roget's Thesaurus* had been ripped up and the torn pages were scattered over the linoleum. I looked out of the window and saw the bulky figure moving in the shadows in the street below. Was it Lord Weidenfeld or was I becoming paranoid?

My MI5 gold membership card arrived next morning. In the following weeks I tried to act normally. At publishers' parties the conversation seemed particularly strained and brittle. It was as if everyone had something to hide. I could not help wondering if they were all members of MI5 and all writing their memoirs.

d   The numbers attending our Creative Writing classes began to dwindle alarmingly. Frisby-Leacock stopped coming and somebody said he had gone 'into paperback'.

Word reached me that old Ferdy Hoskins had visited the Frankfurt Book Fair and had been 'turned.' They said he had gone over to Penguin. He was in hiding somewhere under a *nom de plume* and we wondered if he would suddenly reappear one day at a Hatchards signing.

I kept my usual appointment with Control at a Foyles literary lunch.

'Whatever happened to old Jeremy Carshalton?' I asked.

Control looked grim and paused for a full thirty-five seconds before he muttered the single, fateful word: 'Remaindered.'

'God, publishing is a filthy business,' I said bitterly.

Nothing much happened for the next few weeks except that late one night in Whitehall a man with a jutting jaw jumped out from a doorway and attacked me with a briefcase. I assumed that he was a heavy from Sidgwick and Jackson.

Then, the morning after attending the launch of *The Freezer and Microwave Cookbook of an Edwardian Gentlewoman*, I woke up in a sweating agony with stomach cramps. Another attempt had been made on my life.

I acted quickly, taking my thirty-five-page manuscript and hiding it where it would not be found, among the non-sexist children's books at Brent library. In my book I had already been able to name the Fifth Man as Adrian Mole, having acquired a copy of his secret diary.

I took the train to Harrow and Wealdstone to see Frieda, a retired literary editor who knew all the secrets of the publishing circus. I heard her coughing as she unfastened the five bolts and chains on her front door. She was still on sixty extra-strong cigarettes a day.

'Someone is trying to poison me,' I said.

'Don't worry, duckie,' she replied. 'They always serve that frightful white wine at publishers' parties.'

77

Give a ghoul a break

As you probably know, I was appointed some time ago as chairperson of an advisory committee drawing up guidelines on the celebration of Hallowe'en. Our brief was to consider whether it was permissible, in a country at ease with itself, for people to frighten each other out of their wits. In other words, we were looking at ways in which haunting could be non-threatening.

Our preliminary report is published today, just in time for Hallowe'en on Thursday, and is entitled *Towards a More Caring Approach to Making the Flesh Creep in the Nineties and Beyond*. No doubt it will come to be known as the Ghouls' Charter.

My committee devoted many hours to discussing the role of witches. It was agreed that the usual stereotype image of a witch represented a negative portrayal of women. In particular, it was thought unacceptable that witches should be seen to have broomsticks, thus associating them (and women in general) with domestic work. We have recommended that, in future, witches should be depicted with laptop computers.

It was agreed that harm could be done if children thought of witches as ugly crones in rags. 'Today's witch,' our report states, 'is more likely to be an independent woman in a business suit holding down a responsible executive job.'

Witches' blackened, stumpy (and missing) teeth should also be phased out as soon as possible and made illegal by the end of next year. These have been shown to have a bad influence on persons in the seven to fourteen age group on the matter of dental hygiene.

On the subject of fangs, we believe that much more stringent safety regulations should be drawn up to ensure that people do not, in moments of excitement, swallow their own fangs. We hope to produce more detailed recommendations on this subject in due course. There should be less emphasis on vampires sucking their victims' blood, as this does not give sufficient weight to the valuable part played by vegetarians in our society. Also, this could perpetuate the attitude that bats in general are somehow not 'user friendly'.

My committee received many representations about pumpkins. There is a widespread view that, because of their yellow skin and narrow-cut eyes, these pumpkin 'heads' could be taken to be grotesque caricatures of oriental people. We suggest pumpkin monitors be appointed, with powers to search premises and confiscate any of these artefacts that might cause offence. The role of the pumpkin is, in any case, being reconsidered. The October surge in demand has lately been causing distortions in the EC agriculture sector and it has been proposed that after 1992 pumpkins for Hallowe'en will be replaced initially by courgettes and later by globe artichokes, which are expected to be in surplus. This remains to be ratified at the Maastricht summit.

Above all, my committee feels that there should be a massive educational programme to get people to enjoy Hallowe'en in a responsible and safe way. We suggest a huge publicity campaign with the slogan 'Hallowe'en – Don't Die of Fright'. Blood curdling screams should be banned and replaced by some line such as 'whooooo – there is no cause for alarm.' Finally, as this is now a classless society, from now on he is plain Mr Dracula.

78

Bad case of the freebie jeebies

Here is a ghost story for Hallowe'en. I hope readers will not be too alarmed . . .

The Tory MP rose from his armchair, went over to the fireplace and kicked the log which was dying in the grate so that the sparks flew up, briefly illuminating the agonised expression on the poor devil's face. I refilled my pipe and leaned back, waiting for his tale to unfold.

'I must relate to you, my dear sir, a most extraordinary occurrence which I would not have believed myself had I not witnessed it with my own eyes,' he began. 'It was on a night towards the end of September. I slept but fitfully, being concerned with the cares of my constituents and of the industrialists it is my lot to advise. Suddenly I was awakened by a rattling sound, as if of a letterbox. Momentarily, I felt a strange and eerie cold draught. Summoning every ounce of my courage, I went downstairs to investigate.'

A look of horror came over my companion's face at the recollection of the incident. He had to take another sip of Remy Martin before he could continue. 'There it was,' he said in a strangled voice. 'A long white envelope had manifested itself on my doormat. The words "By Hand" were written on it, but what sinister hand could have brought it? Feverishly, I tore open the envelope and inside I found a cheque, payable to me, for the sum of £20,000, and signed on behalf of the International Bulldozer and Weapons Systems Corporation of Ohio.'

The Tory MP mopped his brow. 'How could this apparently harmless cheque give off such an overpowering sense of Evil? I could not tell, but I vowed there and then not to allow it to fall into the hands of anyone it might harm. I resolved to send it to a secret bank account abroad. Until this day, I have not mentioned this matter to another living soul. You see, this was, for me, the final proof that I was haunted.'

I drew thoughtfully on my briar. 'There is a tradition round these parts that, whenever your wife is away in the country, you are visited by a young woman,' I mused.

'That would be the Lady in White,' he replied. 'The ghost of some unhappy wretch forced to wander this house. She has appeared on many occasions on the upper floor, in the bedroom or the bathroom. Perhaps she is searching for something, but who knows what? A paracetamol? A Strepsil?'

'Some folk say she is Ms Fiona Fandango, a practitioner in public relations and media affairs,' I ventured.

'It would not do for us to delve too deeply,' the MP replied. 'We should let this troubled soul rest in peace.'

By the light of the dying embers of the fire, he poured out his heart about other unexplained phenomena – the airline tickets that suddenly appeared on the antique desk in the study, the brand new set of golf clubs in the hall, the evening he came home to find the whole of his house mysteriously recarpeted.

'Have you ever felt yourself to be possessed?' he asked, his eyes searching my face anxiously.

'It happened to me,' he continued. 'Last time there was a vote on a proposed increase in MPs' salaries. I was firmly of the opinion that it was inappropriate at the time and I was determined to vote against it. However, some extraordinary malign force overpowered me and somehow *propelled* me into the wrong voting lobby. It was appalling.' He buried his face in his hands and sobs shook his body.

'At first I thought I was ill, that it was a bad oyster I had unwisely consumed at the weekend seminar in Le Touquet on The Role of Parliament in the Future of the Fruit Machine Industry, then I realised that Darker Forces were at work.'

'And now, I understand, you are going abroad,' I said.

'Yes, I must find the answer to these great mysteries that have been troubling me, so I am going on a pilgrimage to the Seychelles, for I am informed that there is a wise old holy man there who may be able to explain all to me.'

'I most earnestly hope that you may find some peace,' I told him.

November

Pouring tea on troubled waters

The fact that we are now on a war footing with the United States over the Gatt talks gives special relevance to my forthcoming book dealing with an earlier instance of trade sanctions imposed by Americans. This was the Boston Tea Party in 1773 when the colonists threw a cargo of East India Company tea off a ship in Boston Harbour. It led to the American War of Independence, with all the regrettable consequences that we now see.

The publication of my book will coincide with the celebrations of the 219th anniversary of the Boston Tea Party on December 16. It is a searing indictment of the men who rowed out to that ship on that infamous night.

The book is called *The Cup that Shames*. I have also scripted a TV drama-documentary called *Dregs*, which may be transmitted by BBC2. I am confident that the event will receive more publicity than the 500th anniversary of the 'discovery' of America by Columbus. I argue that the Boston Tea Party was an act of monumental political incorrectness and those who took part in it make Christopher Columbus look like a philanthropist who enjoyed messing about in boats. Here are some of the charges that appear in the book:

The Boston Tea Party was a major environmental crime. Experts have told me that, in its way, the tipping of all that tea into Boston Harbour may have been an act of pollution almost comparable to the *Exxon Valdez* oil spillage. There were long-term effects, apart from soggy tea leaves silting up the mouth of the Charles River.

All that tea released a large amount of tannin in the water, which almost certainly had a detrimental effect on the marine life. Many people now believe that the population of flounders may have been decimated. Other fish, it is thought, became addicted to tea and went mad from withdrawal symptoms when deprived of further doses. These symptoms were passed on to the birds feeding on the fish. This probably explains the strain of neurotic gulls now found on the eastern seaboard.

Levels of caffeine in the water would also have been substantially increased by the infusion of tea in the harbour. Recent experiments have shown that, after exposure to doses of caffeine, algae become agitated and hyperactive. And barnacles are so disturbed that they become unstuck from their rocks or the hulls of ships. Those men who clambered up the side of the tea ship at dead of night on December 16, 1773, were not just taking the first steps in the American War of Independence; they were unleashing an Armageddon in the ecosystem of Boston Harbour.

Accounts of the Boston Tea Party say that the men who took part were dressed as Red Indians. One hardly knows where to begin the list of charges. Presumably they stole these costumes from the Native Americans. It may be they did this to pass the blame for their exploits on to the Native Americans. My own theory is that what happened on that night of December 16, 1773, was in fact the Boston Fancy Dress Party That Went Horribly Wrong. After consuming considerable amounts of something stronger than tea, these men went on the rampage and boarded the ship.

80

It's not critic

Another twelve months have passed and still the call has not come. Round about the beginning of November my hopes start to rise, and round about now I realise that I am going to be disappointed again. Once more, inexplicably, I have not been asked to name my choice as Book of the Year.

As usual, I made my preparations in good time. In February I managed to get through *A Period of Readjustment; Crisis in the Cameroon Economy, 1974*. I note that in my diary I thought that it was 'flawed but compelling'. In May I was coming round in favour of *Eels Never Laugh*, the early lyric poems of Huang Yu.

In August my wife kindly read *The History of Bootlaces* on my behalf and said she was sure I would have enjoyed it, and she would not mind at all if I nominated it. Neighbours who heard me mentioning that I was probably in the running to make a choice also came round to the house with their suggestions. Later, in August, I was in a rather skittish mood and was seriously considering choosing the *Beano Annual*, just as a piece of intellectual mischief.

In early September I was ready to plump for Dave Warburton's powerful, angry, semi-autobiographical novel, *It's a Fix*, about a lecturer in a northern polytechnic who goes to enormous lengths to be invited to select his Book of the Year, but is thwarted at every turn by the academic and literary establishment.

All this reading was in vain. No invitation came from the literary editors to join their fraternity of the great and the well-read. I am sure it is just a question of making the initial breakthrough; get on the lists and then I will be nominating every year for ever.

I would not go all the way with Dave Warburton and suggest that the whole thing is rigged by a literary freemasonry that has cornered the market in Book of the Year selections, but it does occur to me that if I give over this column to the subject and invite certain people to contribute, then I will start getting invitations from people who hope to be asked to offer their choices next year. If you see what I mean. So here are the nominations of my panel of experts:

Dave Warburton, author and lecturer in Modern British Paperbacks at Halifax Polytechnic: For sheer knockabout comedy I would have to choose *Great Booker Prize Disasters*, an absolutely hilarious collection of the funniest moments on a panel of literary prize judges. At the same time it would be invidious not to mention Oliver Pritchett's novella, *Don't Blame the Shepherd's Pie*, an understated account of a weekend spent as guest of a lecturer at a northern polytechnic.

J. H. Rawlings, Esq, bank manager: Poetry means a great deal to me, and this year I have much enjoyed re-reading Schlammer's great epic, *Rauchen Verboten*, with its utterly convincing portrayal of a sensitive bank manager. It has also been a great pleasure to dip into *The Pritchett–Rawlings Letters, April to July 1987*, a saga of high hopes and low farce, which I hope will eventually be more widely available.

Chloe Delight, actress and model: I have been wrestling with Samuel Beckett again this year, but for sheer drama I would have to select *Adventures in the Cocoa Futures Market*, by that brilliant young financier Adrian Fuse.

Adrian Fuse, commodity broker: Taking a forward position as I do, I am choosing a book for 1988 that has not yet been published. It is a splendid coffee-table volume of colour photographs of high-tech office furniture and features that classic English beauty Chloe Delight.

Simon Truffle, restaurateur: No question about it, *The Good Restaurant Guide*. Page 146 is particularly gratifying.

Professor Lionel Abacus, economist: It is a great disappointment to me that there were no decent books this year about the Cameroon Economic Crisis of 1974. The single effort that was published was sadly superficial. In fact, I found it somewhat less illuminating than the *Beano Annual*.

R. Q. Treadwell, critic and lawnmower repairer: For me,

the most illuminating book of the year was *Choices 1968*. This is an anthology of Book-of-the-Year choices collected from all the serious newspapers and journals of 1968. There are fascinating inter-relations between the characters and their choices, several surprises and, of course, plenty of old favourites like A. J. Ayer, Kingsley Amis, Margaret Drabble and Marghanita Laski.

Roderick Saffron Walden, bishop: At last! In *If You Knew Suzuki* we finally have a comprehensive and comprehensible guide to motorcycle maintenance. Beautifully illustrated and a real *vade-mecum*.

Sebastian Carp, third division footballer with cartilage trouble: *The A to Z of Book-of-the-Year Selectors* was, for me, marred by the absence of my name from it. Therefore I must plump for *It's a Fix*, Dave Warburton's searing indictment of the literary editors' mafia.

Lord Ongar, Liberal whip: I have been hugely enjoying the collection of recipes for cooking stoat compiled in 1744 by my ancestor, the second Baron Ongar – or 'Casserole Charlie' as he was affectionately known. This has been printed and published privately, but is available to anyone who writes to Ongar Hall sending £16.45, including postage and packing. Please mark envelopes 'stoat' in top right-hand corner.

Zed Zedkins, rock star, philanthropist and conservationist: I was absolutely knocked out by *Eels Never Laugh*, the collection of poems by Huang Yu that was lent to me by Oliver Pritchett. I have now been able to set these wonderful poems to music and the record is to be issued on the Chiaroscuro label next March.

Simon Truefitt, Conservative MP: Like everybody else I was quite unable to put down the utterly riveting *Eurotunnel Share Issue Prospectus*, which I thought was altogether a better read than the *BP Share Issue Prospectus*. However, in the end, I felt I must go for *It's a Fix*, which was written by a constituent of mine, Mr Dave Warburton. The novel gives a brilliant account of how Mrs Thatcher's Government has brought prosperity to Halifax and re-vitalised the polytechnics in the North of England.

81

And now, the award for the best award

My panel of judges and I were keenly interested in the week-end's Bafta television advertising awards ceremony.

This was the occasion at the Royal Albert Hall at which Maureen Lipman was named best actress for her performance as Beattie in the BT commercials, Rowan Atkinson was best actor, as that man without a Barclaycard, and the Esso Tiger saw off the challenge of the Andrex labrador puppy.

It so happens that I am this year's president of Baaca, the British Academy of Awards Ceremony Arts. There are so many awards ceremonies nowadays, and they have become an art form in themselves. Our academy was set up to foster excellence in these ceremonies. My fellow judges and I are at this moment considering nominations for those who will be presented with the coveted 'Backy' at our own star-studded award ceremony, to be held next year in the ballroom of a posh hotel in Park Lane.

A Backy, incidentally, is a bronze statuette of a weeping man holding aloft a statuette of a weeping woman. Although it is not really allowed, I thought I would give you a clue as to some of the probable winners this year.

The Backy for the Best Prawn Cocktail at an Awards Cere-mony Dinner is likely to be carried off once again by the Empress Motel, just outside Derby. This was the venue for the annual dinner and prize-giving of the British Lettuce Shredders Guild.

We have had to consider a record number of nominations for Best Satellite Link-Up with Recipient Who is Unable to be Present Tonight. My own feeling is that the well-tried formula of the winner being filmed beside her swimming pool in Los Angeles, or in her dressing room at some West End theatre, has had its day. That is why I am confident that the award this year will go to the legendary Dave Bishop.

When Dave was named Most Courteous Milkman in Wiltshire he made his acceptance speech 'live' from a *different* awards ceremony, 500 miles away, where he had been nominated in the Son-in-Law of the Year contest sponsored by a firm manufacturing bathroom tiles. The brilliant twist was that, in the end, he did not actually win the Son-in-Law award.

The prize for the Longest Walk to Collect an Award is almost certain to be won by Tessa Scrimshawe. When she was named Best Supporting Actress in a Radio Commercial for a Building Society, at a gala dinner last March, she took no less than twenty-four minutes and nineteen seconds to make her way from her table at the far end of the ballroom where the event was held to the platform to collect her statuette. She was applauded all the way.

On her journey she kissed 139 friends and well-wishers, shook hands with sixteen influential directors, paused at another table to finish the peach melba belonging to a rival she had defeated for the award, and signed up with a new agent.

At our own Baaca awards dinner we propose to seat Tessa at a table right next to the platform.

Anybody who watched the televised awards ceremony marking the Year of Achievement in Lawn Mower Maintenance will agree that Eugene Theakston, who won the Most Promising Newcomer category, is the man to beat for the Baaca award for Most Drunken and Surly Acceptance Speech.

The adorable Miss Trixie Zabaglione, who presented the prizes for the British Academy of Conjurors' Assistants, is my bet to be named Most Scatty and Bubbly Awards Hostess. Although some of the other nominees wore even more precarious ball gowns, and although Trixie may have let herself down a little by being able to read some of the words and names on the card, she performed one memorable feat.

When it came to presenting the award for Best Solo Performance with Doves, Trixie, in a moment of most endearing confusion, embraced the award (an 8 in. piece of abstract sculpture), then picked up the recipient and handed her over to the MC.

As president this year, it falls to me to present the Arthur F. Thrimble award for a Lifetime's Achievement in Awards Ceremonies. It will go to M & G Stationery Supplies, which has been providing (at a discount) the envelopes and cards for nominations for more than twenty-five years.

As I present it, I hope to receive an accolade myself – for Most Embarrassingly Over The Top Tribute.

82

More sinned against than Cinderella

The ball was a total and absolute fiasco. I can tell you that it is definitely the last time I accept an invite from HRH Prince Charming. *Quel drag!* The whole affair was supposed to end with a terrific firework display at 2 a.m., but instead the proceedings came to an unseemly halt round about midnight.

I may add that the young lady who caused this shambles by dashing out of the ballroom in a rather exhibitionist way had also arrived quite unnecessarily late in the first place.

It started promisingly. Old Baron Hardup was there, of course, with his new wife. A gloomy fellow, but a good sort really. Naturally, he tried to buttonhole me and get me to come in on his latest business venture. Some ridiculous scheme to open a chain of fast-food outlets called Pumpkin-U-Like. I am afraid Hardup isn't really cut out to be an entrepreneur. I managed to off-load him onto my accountant's wife, who began to get a glazed look after twenty-five minutes of his earnest sales talk.

That silly ass Buttons had managed to inveigle his way into the thrash. I don't know how he gets away with it. The man is a crashing bore. All those dreadful saloon-bar jokes. He actually tried out that old there's-a-hole-in-my-bucket routine on me. What a nerve! I made an excuse and headed for the avocado dip.

I bumped into Baron Hardup's two stepdaughters and we had some jolly talk. Those sisters may not be much to look at but they are awfully good value. Their dresses were absolutely *outrageous*.

It was soon after this that the Young Thing arrived. Well! She was dressed in some frothy white number and she swept up to the palace in a gold coach with six white horses, a rat-faced coachman and two lizard-eyed footmen. I must say I thought the gold coach was a bit OTT. Even the smartest people are satisfied with an environment-friendly barouche these days.

'Don't you think that degree of ostentation is just teensy bit *nouveau*?' I remarked to Prince Charming, but I am not sure that he caught my drift.

Curiosity got the better of me and I shimmied over to her for a bit of chat. Five minutes' conversation with her was like five years' hard labour.

'So, how do you occupy your time?' I murmured suavely.

'Housework, mostly.'

Ye godmothers! This was hardly what you would call a promising start. With so many career opportunities for women, you expect a bit more than this. I was mystified, because, with a gold coach, white horses, coachman and footmen she was obviously not short of a bob or two. Surely she would have staff to do all the washing and dusting.

'And what aspect of housework do you find most demanding?' I asked. You can tell I was working hard.

'Clearing out the grate.'

Well, I had a brave try at drawing her into a conversation about the relative merits of open fires and central heating and fuel bills and so on, but I didn't have much joy. I told her the saga of my night-storage heater, but she wasn't really concentrating. She kept asking me what time it was.

Thank goodness, Prince Charming came along and took her off my hands. He was obviously smitten. Not a very bright fellow. A bit of a hooray.

It was at midnight that the disaster occurred. Suddenly this girl gave a little yelp and dashed out of the ballroom. All the rest of us guessed at once what the explanation was. Salmonella. And the finger of suspicion pointed at the vol-au-vents. There was a general discreet movement towards the door.

In the crush on the stairs, I tripped over something. It was a small shoe. A glass slipper, in fact. This was jolly dangerous. You could get a nasty cut if you fell over it and it smashed. It was unforgivable to leave it lying around like that.

'Whomsoever this shoe fits ought to be prosecuted,' I said

to Prince Charming. He took the offending footwear from me and wandered off looking vague.

And you won't believe what I saw next. Mice. Six of them. The palace is clearly infested. It's not surprising that the girl got food poisoning. Worse was to come. I was just going out of the palace gates when I fell over some large, round object. When I picked myself up, my dinner jacket was covered with squishy pumpkin. One thing is certain. Next time Prince Charming gives a party I shall *not* go to the ball.

83

Home is where the art is

As November draws to a close, I always receive hundreds of letters from readers asking for advice on choosing upmarket 'arty' Christmas cards. I thought it might be helpful this year to give an outline of the history of Christmas card art, mentioning some of the 'greats' of the greetings world.

The second half of the twentieth century has seen a rapid expansion in the number of Christmas cards sent, which is why the period has come to be known as the Renaissance. Artists working away in comparative obscurity suddenly achieved recognition. In Florence, Rome and Venice, artists were giving us such classic works as *Madonna on Recycled Paper* and *The Unicef Madonna* and *The Nativity in Pack of Five with Envelopes*.

In this period Brueghel was producing some of his finest work, in particular the busy snow scene now popularly known as *With Sincere Good Wishes for a Happy Christmas and a Prosperous New Year*. This is thought to have been commissioned (circa 1974) by Mr Philip Plasket (the Elder), a prosperous Nuneaton merchant. Students of Brueghel's cards believe they have identified Mr Plasket in the picture. He is the stooped figure on the left, wrapped in the heavy scarf that was probably given to him by his sister Enid (partially obscured by tree in right background).

It is surprising that the Impressionists never became involved in the Christmas Card Movement. They remained in a cultural backwater, devoting all their energies towards a form of card art known as Blank for Special Messages. It is believed that Renoir tried his hand at a series of coaching scenes but they never 'came off'. He was dissatisfied with his seasonal attempt at a group of angels with trumpets and changed it to a group of angelic young women with umbrellas. Monet's somewhat feeble effort to produce a traditional hunting scene had to be rescued and turned into a field of poppies.

In spite of this, all the Impressionists were most conscientious about sending each other cards at Christmas. Recently a card sent by Degas to Manet was discovered in an attic in Paris. The picture was entitled *Petit Oiseau (Rouge-Gorge) dans la Neige*.

84

A very early fog followed by more persistent reigns

Many people will have been surprised by the report in yesterday's *Telegraph* that this has been the mildest November since records began in 1659. Surely, they thought, records began much earlier than that. Of course, an interest in the weather goes back further than 1659, but that was, indeed, a significant date – as I have shown in my recent book *Heavy at Times*, which is a scholarly history of British weather.

The date of the Restoration, when Charles II came to the throne after the end of the Cromwellian Protectorate, was 1660. But 1659 was a more important year, as this was when weather forecasting and the keeping of records were restored.

Obviously, the Puritans outlawed meteorological research, considering it frivolous and linked to superstition. You could be disembowelled for hanging a piece of seaweed on a nail outside your house. A farmer whose cows were seen to lie down could be found guilty of 'the vile and ungodly practice of forecasting' and have one-fifth of his property confiscated.

Before Cromwell, Charles I was a fairly good but unreliable supporter of weatherpersons; they referred to his time on the throne as 'the patchy reign'. Charles II gave enthusiastic encouragement, and his was known as 'the more persistent reign'. He was called the Meteorological Monarch.

It was, in fact, a common interest in the weather that drew Charles and Nell Gwynn together. The King saw her selling oranges in Drury Lane and remarked: 'Upon my soul, I never expected to see oranges ripen in England at this time.'

Nell replied: ' 'Tis the recent spell of mild weather, Sire. The mildest November since records began a few years ago.'

The King said you never knew where you were with English weather, and Nell replied: 'Too true.' The King said you put

240

on a thick doublet first thing in the morning, when you thought it might turn out chilly, and then you regretted it by lunchtime.

Nell said the seasons seemed to have got all mixed up, and Charles said he blamed it on Isaac Newton and all that scientific meddling with nature. Nell said you couldn't rely on what the forecasters said any more, and Charles said he would not bet on a white Christmas.

Records of the weather were actually kept by monks in the fifteenth and sixteenth centuries, but all the devices for measuring temperatures and all the illuminated manuscripts recording mild Novembers and unseasonably wet summers were destroyed in the Dissolution of the Monasteries.

Although Henry VIII was undoubtedly annoyed at the Church of Rome, some historians (including myself) now believe that the Dissolution of the Monasteries came about because of a disagreement over the weather.

There is a story that in June, 1535, Henry VIII remarked: 'It is uncommonly hot today.' An impertinent abbot replied: 'Not so uncommonly hot, actually. Records show that in June, 1532, average temperatures were much higher. And even in April 1531 there were hotter days than this.'

It was then that the King decided that the monasteries would have to go.

In Shakespeare's day weather forecasters were great celebrities. The masses were fascinated by characters like Master Kettley and Mistress Charlton who would appear at public entertainments, such as bear-baiting, or at performances at the Globe Theatre, and predict what the weather would do. They carried symbols – black and white clouds, suns and flashes of lightning – and they would juggle with these to illustrate their forecasts.

In those days, a weatherperson might appear in, say, the West Country, and forecast light rain spreading to East Anglia by nightfall, then he would have to go on horseback as fast as he could to Norwich to deliver this bulletin before the rain arrived. If the wet weather beat him to it, he would be lynched by the local populace.

In November 1609, the erratic behaviour of a ridge of high pressure over the Azores led to such unpredictable weather conditions that no fewer than 560 forecasters were put to death by outraged members of the public. Their heads were cut off, stuck on the end of stakes and left out in all weathers. It was not until the glorious year of 1659 that meteorology fully recovered and records began again.

December

85

Anybody for second helpings?

Today I am giving you my foolproof method of preparing the traditional Christmas turkey. What you will need: four ounces of butter, one pound of salt, a sheet of silver foil, approx three metres by eight metres, a larding needle, a box of crackers, a bottle of dry white wine, a chair and one pound of brazil nuts. Also, as all recipes say, freshly milled black pepper. This last ingredient has often puzzled my readers. How, they ask me, could you have stalely milled black pepper?

This betrays a basic misunderstanding of cookery and cookery writing: the word 'freshly', refers to the *manner* in which you turn the top of the pepper-mill. In other words, you must do it freshly, not lethargically, moodily, indolently, casually, etc. You will also require a turkey.

Timing is all-important. Make sure you have a strict schedule and stick to it religiously. One useful tip here: for a 10–12lb turkey allow twenty-three minutes longer than the cooking-time shown in the recipe book and for a 12–15lb turkey allow an extra thirty-seven minutes.

Here is the timetable if you are planning to have your Christmas meal at lunchtime. Get up at 5 a.m. to put the oven on at gas mark 7 and to chill the wine. Go back to bed. Get up at 6 a.m. to check that you did not just dream you put the oven on. Go back to bed. Put the bird in the oven at 7 a.m. after first wrapping it loosely in silver foil. The leftover six metres of ripped and shredded silver foil can be used to decorate the Christmas tree or to stuff in draughty cracks in the kitchen window. When you parcel the bird in foil make sure to leave a fair sized hole in it so that other members of the family can peer through it and say: 'It doesn't seem to be doing anything at all.'

After thirty minutes take the turkey from the oven and remove the giblets and put in the stuffing you had forgotten. Turn the oven down to gas mark 3. Have a glass of wine.

From now on it is plain sailing. However, you must remember to take the roasting tin out of the oven from time to time in order to baste your shoes. Put the four ounces of butter on a plate conveniently close to the stove for treating burns and scalds. Have a glass of wine.

An hour later members of the family will start to become impatient. You can check for impatience by timing how often they come into the kitchen offering to 'help'. When the offers of help come every three minutes, take the box of crackers and, using the larding needle, carefully remove the novelty from one cracker without damaging the cracker itself. Suggest that the family amuse themselves by pulling crackers while they wait, in the dining room. Allow thirty-five minutes for crawling round the floor looking for the missing novelty.

Now take the chair, wipe it with a damp cloth and wedge it under the handle of the kitchen door to keep out intruders. Baste your shoes again. Have a glass of wine.

At 2 p.m. you will hear a sizzling and seething noise. This indicates that the family's impatience has turned to semi-violent rebellion. Send them some brazil nuts, but no nut-crackers. Allow forty-five minutes for working out how to open nuts without nut-crackers. Have a glass of wine. Decide not to bother about gravy.

When you think the turkey ought to be ready, pierce the thickest part of the thigh with a skewer. If you feel no pain the turkey is cooked. Remove it from the roasting tin but be prepared for the tidal wave of hot fat which will gush from the open end of the bird. Put your shoes and socks in the dustbin. Finish the wine. Take one pound of salt and scatter it over the floor to avoid skidding in congealing fat. Freshly mill some pepper over it to cheer yourself up.

Many cooks I know also like to throw the bread sauce onto the floor at this stage. This can produce a very attractive effect. One word of caution, though: try to avoid stepping on the onion from the sauce as the cloves in it can be quite sharp and can injure your bare feet.

Now everything is almost ready at last. All you have to do

is put the turkey in a draught-free place to 'relax' while you dash out of the house and tear round the neighbourhood, hammering on the doors of closed greengrocers' shops and the houses of perfect strangers, to try to track down the brussels sprouts which you forgot to buy.

86

Yuletide voyeur

There is nothing more fascinating than other people's Christmas cards. You are invited into someone's house for a seasonal drink and within seconds you find yourself drawn irresistibly to the mantelpiece, sidling along it surreptitiously with your head cocked trying to peer inside the cards to see who they are from. All the time you are keeping up some sort of pretence of conversation.

Then your elbow catches the rather classy Victorian coaching scene from Peter and Molly, which tips onto the droll snowman from the Perkinses, which dislodges the Turner reproduction from Keith, which knocks over the Virgin and Child from All at Number 32 and the whole lot clatters to the floor in a blizzard of Seasons Greetings. The Yuletide Voyeur is unmasked.

Other unhelpful people dangle their cards on loops of cotton on the wall, so that you can only check them properly by lying on the floor or by bringing the whole lot down, then going through them as you help to pick them up.

Meanwhile, your wife, who is managing to keep up an animated conversation at the other end of the room, is mouthing an urgent secret message to you. After three or four attempts you lip-read the fateful question: 'Where's ours?' You set off to prowl round the room in search of it.

This year you played safe and sent them the Agnostics' Special – the tasteful picture of the Three Wise Men which can be taken as either a religious card or, if preferred, just a colourful ethnic scene. At last you find it. On the bookshelf. Second shelf from the bottom.

You cannot understand this. Surely it is better than Peter and Molly's banal Victorian coaching scene which has pride of precarious place on the mantelpiece. So it is not the quality of the card which counts; it is the status of the sender. Who are Peter and Molly? Almost certainly your host's boss, who is known for the rest of the year as That Mr Abercrombie, but steels himself to be more chummy when he sends out his bulk-bought coaching scenes to middle management on December 15 every year.

So, now you have discovered that you are a second-shelf-from-the-bottom sort of friend. Retaliation is called for. It is petty to knock a fragile bauble off their Christmas tree. Better to return home and demote the card they sent you (a flock of sheep very much like the ones the shepherds might have kept watch over, when the angels appeared to them) to a junior position on top of the refrigerator.

Now That Mr Abercrombie always sends out his Christmas cards on December 15 – it is marked in his secretary's diary – but when do you send out yours? Timing is crucial. If you send them too early it looks as if you are simply soliciting cards in return. If you send them too late it looks more like a Panic Response than a Message of Goodwill.

I have evidence that some people steal out at around midnight on Christmas Eve, creep around the streets and drop Christmas cards through their neighbours' letter-boxes so that it is too late to reciprocate. Wishing you an uneasy Christmas.

Which sort of cards do you send to which sort of people? From Mark and Sybil you receive a charity card printed on recycled paper which depicts a dove with what looks like a sprig of seaweed in its beak and inside there is a plea for World Peace printed in Vietnamese and various other languages in which you are now rusty. Then the realisation dawns on you. This worthy card has crossed in the post with the one you sent to Mark and Sybil. It was a very lush picture of the aftermath of a slaughter – an antique table piled high with dead pheasants, hares and mallard with assorted fruit and veg and a salmon.

Have Mark and Sybil Turned Serious, or is it that they think you have? The Wilkinsons have sent you this card showing a Splendid Father Taking His Two Rosy-Cheeked Well-Wrapped-up Children Ice Skating. Not exactly your idea of Wilkinson family life. Not with those two destructive Wilkinson brats.

The cards are becoming more and more old-fashioned and nostalgic. People in Victorian costume hold lanterns and sing carols outside desirable detached residences; crowds of staff gather outside inns to welcome late arrivals in the horse-drawn coach; free-range turkeys.

We need some modern Christmas scenes – 'Children Peering Expectantly Through the Window Praying for the TV Repair Man to arrive before the *Top of the Pops* Christmas Special'; 'A Deserted Railway Station on Boxing Day'; 'Father and Well-wrapped-up Rosy Cheeked Children Setting out on a Frosty Night to Find a Shop which is Open and Will Sell HP3 Batteries.'

87

Restive season

Dearest Sylvia,

How frightfully efficient you are making plans for Xmas
already! And it's still November! It does creep up on one,
doesn't it? So sweet of you to ask us over, but isn't it Our
Turn to Have You? We *were* just planning to pull up the
drawbridge and have a quiet one – with the 'two naughty
grannies' and poor, dear old Hamish who is still moping about
his divorce, and a couple of gerbils (Abelard and Heloise) that
Sophie is bringing home for the hols.

Humphrey would love to have you and we *long* to see how
Roger's moustache is progressing. How is the 'little terror'
Kevin? Do say you'll come. Fondest love, Deirdre.

PS. That silly business about Trivial Pursuit is *entirely*
forgotten.

Dear Sylvia,

So glad you will come. Yes, of course you can bring Auntie
Sybil. We insist. I remember how she kept us enthralled at
the Christmas of '86 translating sums like 88p and 56p into
'old money'. Also her reminiscences of Hove before it went
'down' socially. I am sure the Doberman will be no problem;
we can shut our spaniel in the garage. She is still very nervous
after the 'bread sauce incident' of '86. Lots of love, Deirdre.

Sylvia my dear,

No, really don't bother to bring mince pies. They'll only
get squashed in the hatchback if Kevin is restless on the long
journey. We still laugh about that salmon mousse! By the way,
please assure young Kevin that I will re-schedule the turkey
so that he can watch his precious video of *Kung Fu Warriors*

from the Swamp. It will give us a chance to have a glass of Chablis and a natter. Love, Deirdre.

Dear Sylvia,

I never knew you had a cousin Edgar! Dying to meet him. Of course Humphrey will pick him up from Hull. With the motorway it won't take more than four hours. What sort of vegetarian food does he like? Love, Deirdre.

Sylvia,

Hurried note to say I don't know Humphrey's shirt collar size. Non-speakers at the moment. Some silly grumble about 'being treated like a chauffeur'. Why not get him colourful socks? I've got Kevin's boxing gloves in the size you said. What big hands he must have! Luv, D.

Dear Sylvia,

Humphrey wonders if Roger has a road map to show him how to get from Hull to pick up your sister-in-law in Brize Norton. He is planning a round trip to drop off presents with his first wife and her 'tribe' in Caerphilly. It means he has two Christmas dinners in one day. Hugs and kisses, Deirdre.

Oh, Sylvia,

Amazing news! Hamish has got a new girlfriend! She's Icelandic, something to do with industrial chemicals, immensely tall and doesn't speak a word of English. We'll meet her at Christmas. Can't wait! D.

Sylvia and Family,

How do you like this Christmas card? Sorry about the snowman and the robin, but it's on recycled paper. A charity card – in aid of dolphins, I think. Absolutely *adored* your Magi! Humphrey says On No Account bring parsnip wine. We still have plenty from last time, the Famous Christmas of '86. Love from us all.

Dearest Sylvia,

What a shame Roger has to go on a business trip over Xmas. He is obviously v. important in the company now. Must be that moustache! Why don't you all stay over and he can join us on the 29th? I am sure we can fit everyone in. Humphrey says he finds it quite comfy sleeping in the garage. See you soon, Deirdre.

Sylvia,

Had to write to say so sorry I burst into tears on the phone last night. It's the build-up – always makes me emotional. I hope it will be all right if your niece, Sharon, sits with the little ones at a separate table. How nervous is her disposition, exactly? And H wants to know if you said Exeter or Exmouth. Yes, do bring sleeping bags. As many as you can muster. Isn't Hamleys hell? Lots of love, Deirdre.

Dear All,

Welcome! Turkey in the freezer, extra blankets in the airing cupboard, parsnip wine in the garage, Humphrey on a motorway somewhere. I will drink a yuletide toast to you in my 'exile' in the Seychelles. Lots of love, must dash to airport, D.

PS. Don't forget to feed the gerbils.

88

Blessed is he who gives: bewildered he who receives

Many people, I know, find it difficult to express gratitude on Christmas Day. At the moment of opening the present they become agonised about what to say. It is not that they are ungrateful, it is just that they have a communication problem. Sometimes it is difficult to put conviction into the words 'just what I've always wanted' when you are holding up a newly-unwrapped pair of grey socks.

Certain philosophical questions start to nag inside you, such as: 'If I've always wanted grey socks why have I never done anything about it? At times when I have woken up in the morning badly wanting grey socks, as usual, why didn't I just go out and buy some? Have I spent my life so far with this deep-felt need for grey socks and just hoped that one day some aunt will oblige? If I am as pathetic as that I don't deserve grey socks. Perhaps I should give them back.'

All this can cause seasonal stress, so it is good news that you can now get counselling and therapy to help you get over such problems. Mrs Gracias Muchos, who describes herself as a qualified Thankologist, has set up an organisation called Recipients Anonymous and she gives treatment at her home in Tring.

Having been lost for words to describe my feelings on receiving some soap-on-a-rope last Christmas, I decided to go along and join the course.

'It's you! How amazing! I don't know how you do it!' Mrs Muchos exclaimed as she opened the door for me. She helped me off with my coat. 'Where did you find this wonderful wrapping? You're so *clever*,' she said, hanging up the coat and continuing to stroke it. 'Glad you like it,' I mumbled.

I handed her a cheque for the £250 fee for the day's course. 'If it's too big I could always change it,' I said.

'No, it's just right. And I love the colour of it. That subdued pink with black printing on it. My absolute favourite.' She held the cheque in both hands and pressed it against her cheek, snuggling it, then waltzed down the hall to the room where a session of Recipients Anonymous was already in progress. 'Look what I've got everybody,' she cried. 'A lovely cheque!' There was a chorus of 'I say!' and 'Lucky you!'

In our first exercise, all of us 'giftees' – as Mrs Muchos called us – were given a parcel which was quite obviously a bottle. Our task was to say 'Now, I wonder what *this* could be' and take at least one minute and thirty-eight seconds to unwrap it while continuing to appear mystified. Those who failed to be credible were made to wrap the bottle up again and repeat the exercise.

Mrs Muchos then asked Muriel, who was obviously the star pupil, to demonstrate the correct reaction to a 'gift identification malfunction.' In other words, she had to respond to a present when she did not know what it was supposed to be. When she took off the paper there was just an empty jar inside. She held it high in the air and produced a small vocal fanfare – 'Ne-nah!' We all clapped.

After that, we spent some time calling out in unison such things as 'Handkerchieves!' and 'William, you *shouldn't* have' and 'Susan, how did you *know*?' and '*The Complete Encyclopaedia of Carburettors* – I've been longing to read this one.'

There was a coffee break after this and by now we had got into the spirit of things. 'These biscuits are incredible!' we shouted. And 'Milk and sugar as well! I don't believe it!' And 'I love the way the cup comes with its own saucer.'

When the coffee break was over we spent the rest of the morning practising saying 'George!' in a tone that was simultaneously reproachful and delighted.

In the afternoon we formed a circle and Patricia stood in the middle. Seven of us, in turn, presented her with identical gift packs of three little pots of jam and she had to react in a different way to each one. After the fourth, she just burst into tears. We all agreed it was a neat touch.

The others were still doing exercises – free associating with glace fruits – when it was time for me to go. Mrs Muchos showed me to the door and then handed me a diploma which said I had reached the required standard of proficiency in accepting gifts. I took it from her. 'Mrs Muchos,' I said, shrugging and shaking my head with an expression of sorrowing helplessness tinged with happiness, 'what can I say?'

89

The greatest of these is subsidiarity

One of the great scandals of our time is the way that humorous columnists have been feather-bedded by, successively, the EEC to EC and the EU.

Brussels has produced a steady flow of regulations, directives and initiatives to keep us in business. We have grown enormously rich on all the largesse dished out by the Eurocrats while we just spread artificial satire all over the place and wait for the next handout of official surrealism.

We are making ho-ho while the sun shines, but I can see trouble ahead. When there is over-production of EU jokes, French humorists will be overturning lorry loads of British puns at Calais, Spanish comic writers will be accused of stealing our best conceits and a whimsy war will break out between Britain and Greece.

Good King Wenceslas looked in. It was on Thursday, shortly after breakfast. When he stuck his head round the door I could tell that he was not a happy monarch. I know December can be a *mensis horribilis*, but Wenceslas was in the depths.

'Look at this,' he said crisply, tossing a thick document across the table to me. It was called *EEC Notes for the Guidance of Persons Proposing to Look Out on the Feast of Stephen*. 'It's from a former page of mine,' he said. 'He bettered himself and got a job in Brussels. He's an official in the EEC Philanthropy Commission.'

I skimmed through the fifteen-part section on safety regulations. 'It's perfectly all right,' I told Wenceslas. 'You'll still be able to look out, provided you fix guard rails to an approved EEC standard round your windows. All it means is that when you call your page hither to stand by you, it will be necessary to ensure that he is wearing a safety harness. And, of course, hard hats are mandatory.'

'We Wenceslases have been looking out for generations and never had any trouble,' he grumbled. 'Now we have to go through this rigmarole.' I explained to him that it would be just the same as ever. He would ask the page for the name and address of yonder peasant and the page would reply: 'Sire, he lives a good 4.828 kilometres hence, underneath the mountain.'

'So then I can just toddle over to him as per usual with the flesh and the wine and the pine logs?' Wenceslas suggested.

'First of all,' I said, consulting the document, 'we have to get more details about the activities of yonder peasant.' We agreed that the winter fuel he was gathering was probably the odd dead branch, rather than dried grasses that were still technically growing, in which case he would be deemed to be engaged in agriculture. So, provided he was not in an area that had been 'overgathered' and provided he had not exceeded his dead-branch quota, it was all plain sailing.

'Just one more thing, GKW,' I said. 'Would this peasant be an economic migrant or an asylum-seeker?' Wenceslas said that, since he and the page would be trudging through the rude wind's wild lament and the bitter weather in order to deliver the goods to the peasant, he imagined it would be classed as on-the-spot aid.

'I take it that you would have a certificate to say that the flesh had been inspected and that it had been kept correctly in a refrigerated condition,' I said, looking up from paragraph 886 of the document. Wenceslas gestured vaguely. Obviously the authorities are not going to be rigid in their interpretation of the regulations. However, they will insist that, in the interests of hygiene, the flesh, wine and pine logs are stored and transported separately. This will mean that he will have to take on two extra pages to do the carrying. Rubber gloves will be worn.

'It says here that no page shall be required to do more than one hour's continuous walking through snow, however deep, crisp and even,' I pointed out.

'And I'm going to have three of them treading in my steps,' he sighed.

258

At this point, GKW had stumbled on one of the most difficult issues involved in the whole Feast of Stephen operation, namely: how dinted is 'dinted'? According to the protocol agreed at the EEC summit in Rouen some months ago, a dint should be no less than 1.33mm deep in order to generate any heat in the very sod. The depth of a dint should not exceed 2.24mm. For this reason, it will be necessary for a team of eight EEC dint inspectors and an independent arbitrator to accompany Wenceslas and his three pages on their mission to yonder peasant.

'So, when we finally bear the flesh and the wine and the logs thither, we can see him dine, can we?' he said.

'Probably,' I replied. 'You may have to levy a fine on him first for not wearing a luminous orange jacket, since evidence from earlier pages suggests it will be after lighting-up time.'

'I've had enough,' Wenceslas groaned. 'I've a good mind to give the whole thing up and go wassailing instead.'

'Don't forget,' I said. 'If you wassail, don't drive.'

90

The Magi Quiz

The question that has been puzzling scholars for centuries is: What did the Three Wise Men do afterwards? I mean, what did they do after they had arrived at the stable and handed over their gifts of gold, frankincense and myrrh? We don't hear any more of them after this.

I have now solved the mystery.

You have to imagine their situation. They would be feeling rather flat. They're tired from their long journey; they've done what they came to do; they're not yet ready to make the trek back home. They sit down on the ground. And now what do they do?

It's obvious when you think about it. They are three wise men and when three wise men are gathered together they try to find out which one is the wisest. They set each other general knowledge tests, brain teasers and puzzles. They give marks for each correct answer. They play word games.

Now you can see that this must be the origin of our own Christmas Quiz. When we sit round the fire today, in the chaos of discarded wrapping paper, trying to tackle all those infuriating problems in the newspapers and magazines we are simply following a tradition started one thousand nine hundred and ninety-five years ago by Caspar, Melchior and Balthazar.

You would be wrong to suppose that these things are put in the paper to take up a bit of space and to distract your attention from the fact that there won't be another paper for a day or so. They date back to that first Christmas.

Many people have asked me what the first Christmas Quiz was actually like. What sort of questions would have been asked? Of course, it is possible that one day, in a cave or a

dried-up river bed, archaeologists may discover the ancient scrolls with the questions on them. Let us hope that they also have the answers, written upside down, at the bottom of the scrolls.

With my expert knowledge of the period and of the area, I can actually reconstruct the situation and give what is probably a quite accurate account of what happened there.

So the Three Wise Men are seated on the ground, and Melchior says: 'Well, that was an absolutely wonderful experience. Now, what shall we do next?'

I imagine that Caspar then gets to his feet and says: 'As a matter of fact I also came bearing a jumbo crossword. I don't know if anybody would be interested?' He fetches the crossword from the saddlebag on his camel, sits down on the ground again and reads out the first clue.

'Five across. Bright light that had a great following. Six and four.'

'Yonder star,' Balthazar replies, with a weary sigh.

'Five down. Another name for Christmas. Eight letters, beginning with Y.'

'Yuletide,' Melchior says in a bored voice.

Being wise men, they find the Jumbo Crossword rather too easy and it is soon finished.

After a certain amount of desultory conversation, Balthazar points out that 'Melchior' is an anagram of 'Rich Mole.'

Caspar adds that it's also an anagram of 'I come H.R.L.'
There is a bit of an argument about this one.

To change the subject, they quiz each other about current affairs, with questions about such things as Herod's childcare policies, about Caesar Augustus and about the new decree that has gone out saying that all the world should be taxed.

At this moment, the shepherds who were at the stable earlier, come past. Balthazar calls after them. 'Hey, how many words of four letters or more can you make from the letters of the word "Bethlehem"?'

'Awfully sorry,' say the shepherds. 'We've got to hurry back to our flocks. Another time, maybe. Must dash.'

'Meet,' says Melchior.

'What?' say the others.

'Meet. A four-letter word from Bethlehem.'

'Theme,' says Balthazar.

'Heel,' says Caspar. 'I say this is great fun. Why don't we meet up every year and do this?'

Melchior, determined to have the last word, says: 'Beetle.'